Books by Lawrence Millman

*Our Like Will Not Be There Again*
*Hero Jesse*
*Parliament of Ravens*
*A Kayak Full of Ghosts*
*Last Places*
*An Evening Among Headhunters*
*Northern Latitudes*
*Paris Was My Paramour*
*Lost in the Arctic*
*Wolverine the Trickster*
*I'll Dream You Alive*
*Fascinating Fungi of New England*
*Hiking to Siberia*
*The Cannibal Lynx*
*At the End of the World*

# *GIANT POLYPORES*
# *&*
# *STONED REINDEER:*

## Rambles in Kingdom Fungi

Second Edition

## Lawrence Millman

Introduction by
Britt Bunyard

Komatik Press
Cambridge, MA
St. John's, Newfounland

Published by
KOMATIK PRESS
rex@komatikpress.com
www.komatikpress.com


ISBN 978-0-9828219-3-0


Printed in the United States of America
Book design by Rex Passion,
Komatik Press
Cover design by Kathie Hodge

# Acknowledgments

Most of the essays in this book have appeared in *Mushroom the Journal, Fungi, The Boston Mycological Club Bulletin, Atlantic Monthly, New Age, Orion, Omphalina,* and The Cornell Mushroom Blog. Of the individuals who have given me myco-help over the years, I'd especially like to thank Leif Ryvarden, Kathie Hodge, Don Pfister, Jim Ginns, Bob Blanchette, Karen Nakasone, and the late Sam Ristich. *Fungi sint semper vobiscum*! I'd also like to thank Rex Passion of Komatik Press for the passion he's put into this book.

All photographs are by the author, except for: *Bully for the Platypus* (Nick Gust), *In Search of an Extinct Fungus* (Tom Murray), *The Noble Polypore* (Tom Volk), *Chaga's Significant Other* (Tuomo Niemela), and *The 2012 Christmas Mushroom Count* (Joe Warfel). The photograph of the author on the back jacket was taken by Lene Zachariassen.

# Contents

# Introduction

"Here's a riddle for you: what's large and furry, more or less hibernates in the winter, and inhabits old growth forests in the Pacific Northwest?"

So begins "The Noble Polypore," one of the essays in this book. You're doubtless thinking that the answer to this riddle is a bear. If so, you'd be wrong. And if you think the furry entity in question is that seldom encountered denizen of the Pacific Northwest commonly called a sasquatch, you'd be wrong again.

But the furry entity is almost as rare as a sasquatch. In fact, fewer than 100 of them have ever been found. Now you're probably scratching your head in bafflement, so I'll give you the answer to the riddle: it's a fungus! Specifically, it's a polypore (bracket fungus) known as *Bridgeoporus nobilissimus*. Especially large specimens can be six feet in diameter and tip the scales at 300 pounds.

"The Noble Polypore" is just one of the many fungi described in *Giant Polypores & Stoned Reindeer* by Lawrence Millman. You can also read about a fungus that infects only platypuses, and only platypuses in Tasmania. You can read about another fungus that the Northern Cree ignite in order to get rid of mosquitos. You can read about fungi that happily grow on dung. You can read not about chaga, but about what Millman calls its "significant other." You can read about...I could go on and enthusiastically on. For the essays in this book are insightful, imaginative, brilliantly-written, and sometimes downright hilarious. What's more, they give the reader an expert window on the mushrooms and other fungi that inhabit our world.

And they do inhabit our world, every part of it. All you need to do is look around you. You may notice mold growing on the leftovers in your refrigerator. As you weed your garden, you might see a large mushroom rising up from among the tulips and daisies. You might find mushrooms in a discarded brassiere (documented in this book!). Now look down at your feet. More than 80 types of fungi make their home there -- some packed on the toenails, others wedged between the toes, and still others at the bottom of the heel. In his "Pre-Ramble," Millman notes that the pillow on which you rest your head at night hosts, at conservative estimate, more than 1,000,000,000 fungal spores.

Yet however ubiquitous fungi might be, they remain enigmatic and distant for most people. But not to author-mycologist Millman. To him, they are at least as interesting as other organisms. And he travels far and wide (often very wide) in search of them. No matter where he finds himself -- in the dwarf birch forests of the Arctic, among headhunters in Borneo, or in a frozen swamp in New England -- he always seems to find weird and unusual fungi. Or, if not weird and unusual fungi, weird and unusual people. In addition to the aforementioned headhunters, this book includes portraits of obsessed British Columbia mushroom hunters, no less obsessed climbers of Everest (yes, there's a fungus on the summit of Everest...), Antarctic explorers, and what Millman refers to as "a mysterious Asian beauty." You'll have to read the book to find out what the last of these is...

I truly envy you, Dear Reader: *Giant Polypores & Stoned Reindeer* is a remarkable book, and you are about to embark on a remarkable journey.


Britt Bunyard
Editor-in-Chief
*Fungi*

# Pre-Ramble

The goal of mycology is to prove itself wrong.

Solve a mycological problem, and you will have created half a dozen more.

Is it a parasite? a saprobe? or a symbiont? To know a fungus, you need to be aware of how it earns its living.

Fungi are a critical lynch-pin in virtually every eco-system.

Look at that large polypore on a stump: it's a worthy elder capable of much wisdom, but only if you listen to it.

Wherever the soil is acidy, fungi make plants possible.

In forest soils, the fungal biomass is 90% of the total organismic weight.

Since fungi like disturbances, you'll find a greater variety of species in a clear-cut than in an old growth forest.

Wi-Fi radiation is an aid to fungal diversity in Holland, where it has increased the number of wood-inhabiting species by causing many trees to shed their bark.

For every fungal compound, there is a mate. One such compound -- norbadione A -- happily bonds with radioactive isotopes, particularly cesium 137.

Less than 10% of all fungi have been identified.

A dry year is usually an excellent year for fungal parasites.

A fungus performs a complex pas de deux of advance and retreat with a host. To call it a disease is a human-centered simplify-cation.

The best myco-medicinal -- a stroll in the woods.

Mycology -- a good walk ruined

Once you start naming things, you see more life around you. By substituting DNA sequencing for taxonomy, many mycologists are losing the ability to see...

Like Garth Brooks, mycologists can say "I got friends in low places." You want an example? Recently, a new fungal genus associated with elk urine-dampened leaf litter was described.

You can remove all the birds and still have a forest, but if you remove all the fungi, the forest will die.Indeed, you could say that the trees in that forest are the photosynthetic appendages of fungi.

The pillow on which you lay your head at night hosts (at conservative estimate) 400,000 spores.

"I will humble you every time," the fungus remarked to me, I thought, a bit condescendingly. Then it added: "But I will also astonish you every time."

# The Thrill of the Hunt

For some people, autumn is a season of melancholy, a time of transience and decay. For me, however, it's the most exhilarating time of year. In autumn, all my senses come alive, my blood quickens, and my adrenaline goes into overdrive. That's because I'm either looking for mushrooms or thinking about looking for mushrooms.

Call it an obsession, or maybe the awakening of a long-dormant hunter-gatherer urge. I put on the most tattered clothes in my wardrobe (sartorial formality, I'm convinced, scares away members of Kingdom Fungi), grab a basket or a paper bag, sometimes enlist a similarly-obsessed friend or two, and off I go.

Instantly, my eyes start scanning the ground. In single-minded pursuit of my quarry, I'll occasionally bump my head against tree limbs, crash into people walking their dogs, come face to face with a black bear, or plunge blindly into a patch of poison ivy. Once I stepped on a nest of yellow jackets and got stung repeatedly, but the discomfort paled beside my delight at finding a large patch of matsutakes. Here I should mention that the matsutake, *Tricholoma magnivelare*, is to other edible mushrooms what Chateaubriand is to a Big Mac.

Upon seeing the contents of my basket, someone I meet on the trail might ask: "Is your insurance paid up?".

After telling the person that I've never gotten sick from eating any of the mushrooms I've gathered, but that I've occasionally become very sick from eating not necessarily fresh cuisine at pricey restaurants, I might then add something like this:

Dear Sir or Madame, try to consider mushrooms as an environmental asset rather than a health hazard. Were it not for their remarkable recycling abilities, the planet would be a heap of rotting vegetable waste. See that crumbling log? It's adding nutrient-rich humus to the soil, thanks to the fungal saprobes inhabiting it. See that red maple, sassafras, or flowering dogwood? Their survival depends on their fungal partners.

Having concluded this short lecture, I move on. I model my pace not after a jogger or a power walker, but after a stout Russian peasant woman in her mushroom-foraging style. Such a woman's typical mode of locomotion, in the words of mycologist Gordon Wasson, consists of "progressing slowly, stooping and peering to the right and the left, with a low, circular, sweeping glance, as though she has lost something." For haste does not make waste so much as it makes for wasted opportunities. Who knows what fungal treasures I might miss if I performed an aerobic stampede through the woods?

I seldom look up even if it's peak foliage time -- an almost religious period in New England. For I'm more likely to see better colors on the ground than the garish scarlets and yellows of turning leaves, which, after all, only indicate dead tissue. For instance, I might have an encounter with the royal blue of a *Lactarius indigo*, the soft purple of a *Cortinarius iodes*, or the bright orange or yellow of a *Hygrocybe* species. On a cherry log, I might find a fruiting of *Trametes (=Pycnoporus) cinnabarinus,* a polypore species whose bright red pores are not so fickle as to change colors with the season.

If there's been a rain, or perhaps a combination of rain and serendipity, the ground might be a veritable blanket of mushrooms. If not, well, at least I will have had the pleasure of nature's company for a while.

Actually, a bad mushroom day -- the result of cold weather, dry conditions, or strong winds sucking moisture out of the ground -- can be fruitful. One chilly November afternoon some years ago, I ventured into the woods with my friend Sam Ristich, one of the Northeast's leading mycologists. Sam, who died in 2008, was a scientist-enthusiast who constantly marveled at the wonders of the fungal world. His car boasted a bumper-sticker that said "I Brake for Fungi."

A not irrelevant aside: Sam wasn't altogether happy with the current tendency among mycologists to regard DNA sequencing as the pinnacle of their trade. For he believed that a fungus is more than the sum of its base pairs, and that the branch it occupies on a phylogenetic tree was perhaps not as important as the branch it might occupy on a real tree. He thought that molecular information, rather than be used exclusively to establish or deny speciation, should be correlated with traditional taxonomy. I agree with him, mostly...

But back to our foray. We weren't finding anything. Nothing at all. No, I lie; on a dead log, we did see a few small mushrooms so desiccated that they could have been virtually anything, and on the ground, there were several *Russula* specimens nibbled ostentatiously by deer or squirrels.

All at once Sam uttered his trademark exclamation of "Hallelujah!" Then he pointed out a large *Narceus* millipede languidly crawling about the leaf litter. An admirable creature, but not a fungus.

Moments later, he exclaimed "Hallelujah!" again. There, on a birch stump, was a kidney-shaped birch polypore (*Piptoporus betulinu*s) -- a quite common species, it's true, but to someone like Sam, even a common species is a miracle, at once an inimitable work of art and a major player in the great carbon cycle of life. In this case, the fruiting body was also thriving with thrips, so Sam, who had trained as an entomologist, was truly in his element.

Sam and I were accompanied by a novice mushroomer named Trish, and on her face was a somewhat dubious expression. Touching the birch polypore's surface, she asked, "Can you eat it?"

"No," Sam replied, "but the Algonquin Indians did use it to get rid of worms."

"I think I'll give it a pass," said Trish.

Once upon a much earlier time, my response would have

been pretty much the same as hers. Almost the only thing I cared about when I beheld a mushroom was whether or not it was edible. Thus I had eyes only for king boletes, morels, blewits, chanterelles, and matsutakes -- everything else was dross, better kicked than picked, better chucked than plucked. I believed (in fact, I still believe) that a mushroom snatched from the wild tastes ten times better -- no, a hundred times better -- than a mushroom procured from a supermarket.

Then one fall day I was walking in the woods outside Concord, Massachusetts, when I had an epiphany. I suddenly thought of the mushrooms I was seeing as an exuberant gallery of shapes and designs, colors and textures. There were umbrellas, gelatinous ears, trumpets, corals, turkey tails, orange rinds, lions' manes, parasols, porcelain vases, crusts, erect phalluses, and even a cauliflower. I could only stand gapemouthed with admiration.

So now, like Sam, I appreciate flagrantly inedible species perhaps even more than I appreciate edible ones. I even appreciate fungal species that would send me on a one-way trip to my Maker. For instance, the so-called Destroying Angel (*Amanita bisporigera*) is one of the most poisonous mushrooms in the world, but it's also one of the most beautiful: a ghostly white apparition rising from the leaf-strewn floor of the forest.

Also, I delight in looking for mushrooms as much as I delight in finding them. When I'm in a foraging mode, I enter a Zen-like state wherein only the hunt itself matters. Anxieties dissipate; my negligible bank balance becomes irrelevant; my physical maladies are cured. I'm not so much pushing at the outer walls of my universe as I am transcending those walls completely. Maybe I'm connecting with my archaic ancestors who lived by the hunt, maybe not. One thing I do know, though -- but for the prospect of mushrooms, my life would be a lot poorer.

And this prospect exists not just in wooded settings, but virtually everywhere. I once drove a beat-up Chevy Nova whose back seat hosted a wide variety of rust and mold species. Some years ago, I lived in a house whose basement seemed to be a magnet for cup fungi. A woman I know once showed me a brassiere that she thought she'd thrown away. Instead of throwing it away, she had left it in a damp place, and it had several inky caps growing inside it. There's a fungus (*Hormoconis resinae*) that can grow in jet fuel by using the alkanes in the fuel as food. And if you find an owl pellet, look at it closely: there might be an *Onygena* species growing on it.

Not too long ago, I happened to be in Death Valley, California. Not a particularly good place for mushrooms, you're probably thinking. But it had rained a couple of days earlier, and in a sand dune near the tourist site known as Scotty's Castle, I chanced upon -- Hallelujah! -- a group of stalked puffballs lifting their heads proudly to the bright desert sky. Water, those doughty fungi seemed to be telling me, is the staff of our lives, too. We snatch it up during those rare times when we see it. Our brown heads and shaggy stalks occupy a place in the earthly firmament no less special than the place you, O sapient person, occupy. It's just that we travel down the river of time with slightly different, slightly quicker paddle strokes than you do. Celebrate us.

# *Collecting for the Table:*
## *A Polemic*

Increasingly, I object to the idea of collecting mushrooms for the table. The table to which I'm referring is not one's dinner table, for I don't object to the harvest of wild edibles. No, I mean the collection tables that occupy pride of place at local and regional forays of several days' duration.

Here's the scenario: a brigade of mushroom hunters lights out for the woods, each of them armed with a capacious basket. Into those baskets they'll toss every specimen they find, then bring back their booty for the foray's experts to sort and identify. The specimens will be accompanied by a dearth of data. What's the substrate? On a tree, the collection notes might say. Whereupon the experts -- often late twenty or early thirty-something males eager to brandish their egos -- will put names on the specimens with such alacrity that they could be tossing confetti. Never mind that many of those specimens can be identified only with the use of a microscope.

The tables in question will have hundreds of paper plates on which the mushrooms rest forlornly while they wait to have names put on them. At a Pennsylvania foray I recently attended, there were perhaps a dozen plates piled high with the same *Boletus* species. If I were a *Boletus* mycelium, I'd be greatly disturbed by this sort of thing. I might even try to evolve a different, scarcely visible fruiting body, to keep it from ending up in such vast quantities on a collection table.

But there's worse to come. All during the foray, the specimens will remain on their plates, becoming "dehydrated, shriveled, and stanched from releasing spores," in the words of mycologist Nicholas Money. In the end, virtually all of them will be dumped into a plastic garbage bag. Not set aside for an herbarium. Not spreading any spores. Not oven-dried for future study. Not even sautéed with onions and garlic. Simply turned into trash. Hardly a fate that any self-respecting mycelium would wish on its creation.

Well, at least that mycelium itself is not disturbed, you might say. But not so fast! For the mycological jury has not yet come up with a verdict on this subject. Truth to tell, much of a mycelium's biomass and an undetermined portion of its energy is transferred to its fruiting bodies, the vehicles for spore production and thus, in effect, its reproductive organs. How would you like it if someone came along and yanked off your reproductive organ? I suspect the mycelium might feel the same way...

To collect or not collect, that is the question. Personally, I think it's nobler to study the objects of one's interest in the field rather than watch them desiccate on a table. And if mycophiles get down and dirty with fungi, they might find out how different species relate to their respective environments. They might also ask themselves some important questions: why, for example, are insects congregating on a certain species? What's the smell of a particular species when fresh? And what the blazes is that tree on which the aforementioned species was growing?

So, please, let's try to collect a little less promiscuously. After all, mushrooms are hardly any different from any other organism, and would you pounce upon every frog, possum, warbler, butterfly, maple sapling, or trillium you see and throw it into a basket? In fact, mushrooms -- more than almost any other organism -- are essential for environmental health, climate control, and the maintenance of biodiversity. Vastly more essential than a certain brash hominid I know...

In the end, too much collecting might mean fewer mushrooms, which could result in less genetic diversity, which in turn might result in even fewer mushrooms. With too few mush-rooms, there's always the possibility that a species might become critically endangered or even extinct. And -- to quote Oscar Wilde -- you don't want to kill the thing you love, do you?

# Travels with Santa and his Reindeer

In the summer of 2003, I was traveling through the Chukotka region in northeastern Siberia, and I happened to eat Santa Claus. Or maybe I should say that I ate the mushroom traditionally eaten by shamans before they become Santa Claus. Or maybe I should just say that the composite figure of Santa Claus includes an anonymous shaman high on a certain mushroom.

Before you accuse me of profaning a popular Christmas icon already profaned by Coca Cola and the poet Clement Moore (author of "The Night Before Christmas"), consider the no less iconic mushroom in question, *Amanita muscaria*, or the Fly Agaric. In its most dramatic color phase, it has a robust red cap with concentric rings of white, wart-like spots on it. Even in its immature button stage, it's still very robust. If it were a human being, you would refer to it as obese.

You might recognize in my description a mushroom depicted in numerous Christmas cards, children's comics, paintings, posters, and stoner websites. Contrary to popular belief, it's not the mushroom depicted in *Alice in Wonderland*, though. If you look at the early illustrations in Lewis Carroll's book, you'll see that the mushroom looks somewhat like a lawn mushroom. Likewise, Alice's trip, taken under the tutelage of the hookah-smoking caterpillar, was more typical of a *Psilocybe* trip than an *A. muscaria* trip. Alice got bigger and smaller, respectively; if she had eaten *A. muscaria*, she probably would have felt like she was flying, as I did.

Gazing at me, Dmitri, my Chukchi companion, said: "With a *wapak* (the Chukchi word for *A. muscaria*), you don't need a ticket or a boarding pass."

Initially, I felt nauseated as well, but nausea comes with the biochemical territory. For while *A. muscaria* contains muscimol, the alkaloid that gave me the illusion of flying, it also contains ibotenic acid, a very potent compound that can give your stomach a turbulent ride. If you dry the mushroom, most of the ibotenic acid decarboxylates (i.e., degrades) into muscimol...most, but not all. Here I should mention that *A. muscaria* has never been implicated in a single death, except in the works of detective writers like Dorothy Sayers (see her novel *The Documents in the Case*, for example).

Dmitri seemed slightly circumspect about eating the mushroom, or at least eating it in public. Part of his reticence probably came from the fact that he was a schoolteacher, and it wouldn't have been appropriate for his students to see him eating this mushroom. But part of it might have been a survival from Stalinist times, when any indigenous person who ate *mukhomor* (the Russian word for *A. muscaria*) would be considered an enemy of the state. Repeat offenders reputedly were herded into airplanes, and when the plane was airborne, the cargo door would be opened.

"You say you can fly," a Stalinist henchman would announce. "Okay -- then fly!"

Whereupon he would push the victim out of the plane.

Meanwhile, the Soviets were flooding Chukotka with cheap vodka, the better to wean the locals from their time-honored traditions. The ritual use of *A. muscaria* might have been a very time-honored tradition: carved into the rock-face near the mouth of the Pegtymal River are a number of Bronze Age petroglyphs that seem to be of shamans whose heads are crowned by *A. muscarias*. The Chukchi refer to these figures as Mushroom People.

According to Dmitri, Chukchi shamans would ingest three dried mushrooms to sustain them during long hours of drumming and singing. As muscimol goes through the human kidneys more or less unaltered, the shaman's acolytes would gather around him and drink his urine. In bad mushroom years, Dmitri said, there was quite a lot of reycling of shamanic urine.

When we encountered an *A. muscaria*, Dmitri gave me precise instructions on how to pick it. Be especially careful with the cap, he told me. If I damaged it, I might end up with some sort of head injury. If I removed the warts from the cap, I would end up losing all of my hair. And if I injured the stem, something unpleasant would happen to one of my legs.

"How unpleasant?" I asked.

"You might need to have the leg amputated," he replied.

Is there any mushroom that's been so anthropomorphized as *A. muscaria*? I wondered while cautiously picking a specimen for later consumption.

In a 1986 article in *The New Scientist*, the English historian Ronald Hutton dismissed the notion that Santa Claus, or Father Christmas, might have been a mushroom-taking Siberian shaman. Such shamans never wore red-and-white clothes, he argues. Nor did they climb in and out of smoke-holes in a trancelike state. Nor were they ever inclined toward gift-giving -- instead, their constituents gave them gifts.

Of course, Santa Claus wasn't a Siberian shaman. To insinuate himself into European folk memory, he would have needed to travel an unconscionably long distance. Likewise, contact with many groups in Siberia didn't occur until well after Santa had done his insinuating.

It would have been much more appropriate for him to enter European lore from a European place, like, for instance, Lapland. In fact, I'd like to propose that Santa, or at least part of him, might have been a Sami (Lapp) shaman. Indeed, Europeans used to regard all Samis as shamans: they believed that the women could curdle milk or give a person smallpox just by thinking about it, and the men could chant away bad weather or disease with their *joiks* (ritual songs).

Only small shreds of traditional Sami culture still survive, but let's go back several hundred years, before Christian missionaries assaulted the Sami way of life. Let's also say that you're a Sami reindeer herder, and that you've taken to your sleeping skins with a mysterious ailment which makes your whole body ache. Through the taiga telegraph, you've put in an urgent call to the local *noaidi* (shaman). Soon the fellow pulls up in front of your lodge in his reindeer-drawn sled, then enters the premises via the smoke-hole. He couldn't have come through the door owing to the pile-up of snow.

"What's wrong with me?" you ask your visitor.

Prior to his visit, the *noaidi* had eaten a few dried *karpassienis* (the Sami word for *A. muscaria*), and he now peers at you with an expression that indicates he's entered a gievvot, or altered state. After a minute or two, he offers his diagnosis of your condition: you've been cursed by one of your neighbors, a guy who seems to think your reindeer are his reindeer.

Damn that little scuzzball, you say to yourself; he'll do anything to get my reindeer.

"But I can get rid of the curse," the *noaidi* tells you.

Stooped over, he starts beating a reindeer chamois *kobda* (drum) ringed with bear teeth and decorated with images of the sun and moon. While he's doing this, he's chanting a joik that consists of certain repeated phrases: *Awaken, O my nature -- O awaken -- go down -- down into the Underworld...* Every once in a while, he leans over and spits on you. Since his saliva contains the healing particles of one or more *karpassienis*, you don't object to what would otherwise be insulting behavior.

Curiously enough, the *noaidi* himself looks like a *karpassieni*. For a shaman who has consumed this mushroom typically turns into a facsimile of it, or at least has taken on its distinctive red-and-white color scheme. Or so the Sami used to believe.

Miraculously, you feel better, considerably better, after the *noaidi's* performance. You rise up from your sleeping skins with the idea of making your curse-wielding neighbor become a resident of his own sleeping skins. At the same time, you feel very grateful to your visitor.

"What a gift you've got!" you inform the *noaidi*.

"Thank the *karpassieni*, not me," he replies. "It transported me to the realm of Jabmiekka, Mistress of the Dead, and she permitted me to retrieve your missing soul, which in turn permitted me to heal you."

After you reward him with some reindeer meat, especially reindeer fat (his ample belly suggests that he's been rewarded in this manner many times before), the *noaidi* clambers back up your lodge's smoke-hole. Soon you hear him whisking off with his reindeer to visit another client.

Here I might mention that Siberians never traveled in reindeer-drawn sleds, a fact that Mr. Hutton points out as well. But the Sami did travel in reindeer-drawn sleds, and some of them continue to do so today. A single reindeer can pull a sled and its driver over a ten-mile course in forty minutes, while a five-dog team will take an hour or more over the same course.

I'd also like to mention that while reindeer will eat almost any mushroom, especially during the fall rut, when they're active seeking protein, they're especially fond of *A. muscaria*. If they eat it, they often end up stumbling around in what would appear to be a stoned manner. For Sami herders, it's not easy trying to move stoned reindeer from one grazing spot to another. Rather than wait until their charges get over the effects of mushroom ingestion, some herders have been known to collect *A. muscaria* fruiting bodies and create trails out of them, the better to make their reindeer go where they want them to go.

No one has interviewed any reindeer about their taste for *A. muscaria*, but if they could talk, I suspect they might say that they quite enjoy the sensation of flying. They might add that a reindeer with a red nose is afflicted with a parasite, usually a bunch of *boaro* (the Sami word for warble-fly larvae), and while the condition can be very painful, even sometimes fatal, it doesn't usually result in one's nose glowing like a light bulb.

Unlike their reindeer, the contemporary Sami seem to have little interest in *A. muscaria*. In the fall of 2005, I was traveling north of Rovaniemi, the administrative capital of Finnish Lapland, and I saw some large fruitings of the mushroom. My Sami companions told me that it was highly poisonous, and they would never eat it. One elderly man added something to this in Davissamegiella, the Sami language. A younger person translated for me:

"He says our *noiadi* used to eat *karpassienis*, and then they would go to other worlds. But that was a long, long time ago."

It's now the night before Christmas, and not a creature is stirring in your house. Not a creature, that is, except for you. You're putting some last minute decorations on a spruce tree that will never reach maturity.

All of a sudden, there's a loud noise in your chimney, and an overweight man with a disheveled white beard lands in the fireplace with a resounding crash. His unusual method of entry suggests that he might be some sort of shaman. Or perhaps a burglar posing as a shaman. After all, a person innocent of any wrongdoing will usually enter a house through the front door rather than the chimney.

"Are you going to rob me?" you ask the fat man.

This idea strikes him as so funny that he bursts into a loud, somewhat vulgar laugh. Then he shows you a bag nearly bursting at the seams.

Truth to tell, your visitor is a hybrid concoction of many diverse parts, some commercialized, some fictionalized, and some reaching into the distant past. While certain aspects of his personality might be inclined to do some shamanizing, other aspects of it would be no more capable of shamanizing than, for example, putting together a weight-watcher's cookbook. The non-shamanic aspects win. So he doesn't spit on you or beat on a reindeer skin drum while chanting in an unknown language. Nor does he seem to be in any sort of altered state, although you can't help but think that he's had a few beers.

The fat man unties his bag, and you see that he's brought all kinds of gifts for you and your family: video games for the kids, a new microwave for the kitchen, Chanel perfumes for your wife, some extremely up-to-date iDevices, and even (this may sound a bit far-fetched) a few books.

You stare at your beneficent visitor, and maybe, just maybe, you might detect in his robust body, not to mention his bright red outfit with white buttons and trimming, a certain robust red-and-white mushroom.

# Mushrooms, Russia and Chauvinism

In their not always accurate book *Mushrooms, Russia and History*, Gordon Wasson and his wife Valentina celebrate Russians as "a people preeminent in mycophagy."

What the Wassons don't say is that this mycophagic preeminence often has its sequel in a preeminent body count, or at least some very preeminent stomach aches. Russians may be eating more mushrooms than anyone else, but they're also eating more of the wrong mushrooms. This has gotten worse in recent years. With so-called democracy, shabby identification skills have become available to all.

On a recent trip to the Arctic archipelago of Svalbard, I visited the Russian coal mining town of Barentsburg (pop. 500). In a small museum devoted to the White Sea settlers known as Pomors, I met a man named Vladimir who became positively radiant when I brought up the subject of *grib* (mushrooms). There were many good edibles a short distance from town, he told me. This statement surprised me, for I was familiar with the range of species in Svalbard, and except for several *Leccinums*, there are almost no decent edibles. The occasional *Russula*, some *Lichenomphalias*, and *Lepista multiformis* (a large brown basidiomycete that fruits in wet tundra polygons), yes; but with respect to edibles...*nyet*.

I asked Vladimir for the names of the species he'd been collecting. He said that he commonly found *lisichkas* (chanterelles) as well as *beliy gribs* (*Boletus edulis*) at this time of year.

I was now highly dubious. Neither species is known from Svalbard, for neither typically grows in a tundra environment. So I asked Vladimir if he would take me to one of the places where he'd been harvesting these two choice edibles. He seemed to have no problem showing me a site. After all, I was an outsider, and thus unlikely to loot his fungal bounty. So we climbed onto his all-terrain vehicle and drove past what I figured was the world's most northerly pig farm, then across several hills devastated by coal mines, and over a dwarf "forest" of six-inch-tall birch (*Betula nana*) and willow (*Salix polaris*).

At last we stopped, and Vladimir pointed to some fruiting bodies in the moss next to a stream. "Look -- *lisichkas*!" he exclaimed.

I looked at the yellowish mushrooms in question. They were *Arrhenias*, probably *A. lobata*, a not uncommon northern moss inhabitor. "Sorry," I told Vladimir, "but those are *Arrhenias*." *Arrhenias* have somewhat cursory gills, which is probably why he made the mistake.

"Very good to eat," he said, obviously thinking *Arrhenia* was the name for chanterelle in my country. Whereupon he began collecting a batch of these non-chanterelles.

Would he become yet another Russian mushroom harvesting statistic (several hundred deaths a year, along with thousands of poisonings) as a result of eating a species whose edibility is usually described as "unknown?" Probably not, since he already seemed to have eaten *Arrhenias*, and he'd lived to tell the tale.

Truth to tell, there are very few *grib* in the Arctic that will land a person in a *grob* (coffin). "Tell me, Vlad," I said, "how do you know these are *lisichkas*?"

He gave me a slightly patronizing look, then thumped his chest and uttered the same two words I'd heard from other preeminent mycophages who shared his ethnic persuasion: "*Ya russkii* [I'm Russian]."

These words rendered irrelevant the fact that *Arrhenias* have gills and chanterelles have ridges. Some years ago, in Cape Cod, they'd also rendered irrelevant the phenol odor of several specimens of *Agaricus meleagris* (a mildly toxic species) in a babushka's basket of otherwise edible *Agaricus*.

To indicate that a Russian might be just as capable of misidentifying a mushroom as anyone else, I mentioned a friend of mine, now resident in the U.S., who had two cousins in St. Petersburg die from eating *Amanitas* in the 1990's. "St. Petersburg! Hah!" was my companion's only comment.

Later I showed Vladimir both *Arrhenias* and chanterelles on the internet, which prompted this response: "Internet is wrong!"

But there is a flipside to this sort of myco-chauvanism, and I'll now give you an example of it. Shortly after Vladimir and I parted company, I found myself standing next to what was probably the northernmost statue of Lenin in the world. On the very top of Lenin's head was a small patch of the sunburst lichen, *Xanthoria elegans*. This yellowish lichen is among the most common fungal entities in Svalbard. A few feet from Lenin, on the ground, was a fruiting of a relatively uncommon mushroom, *Cystoderma arctica*. I was kneeling and photographing the *Cystoderma* when a woman and her two young daughters wandered over to see what I was doing. Soon they were gazing at the mushrooms with the same rapt and doting expressions that their forbears might have reserved for Lenin himself ninety or so years ago.

"*S'edobnyh gribov?*" the woman asked. "Are they edible?" Her look of admiration did not change when I shook my head. One of the little girls said, "*Ya dumauiu, oni krasivye* [I think they're beautiful]."

The woman's expression and her daughter's words reminded me of a statement Valentina Wasson makes in *Mushrooms, Russia and History*: "We Russians love the whole mushroom world…"

Near the end of my visit to Barentsburg, I saw more evidence of the Russian love for mushrooms. Painted on the wall of an abandoned Soviet-era concrete building was a panorama of boletes, *Russulas*, and *Hydnums*, along with several *Amanita muscarias*. There was also a livid green mushroom that possessed only three or four gills. Perhaps a psychedelic *Marasmius*?

It was spitting rain and snow pellets, and a strong wind was whirling through town, so I didn't stop to take any photographs of this panorama of mushrooms. But I did take the mental picture of them described in the previous paragraph. And when I consider that picture, I think to myself, "How impoverished is the graffiti of my homeland…"

# Bully for the Platypus

for Kathie Hodge

Welcome to Tasmania, an island that's part temperate rainforest, part high country wilderness, and part gentle English countryside. This sort of surrealist mingling also defines Tasmania's most celebrated resident, the platypus (*Ornithorhynchus anatinus*). With its duck-like beak, its beaver-like tail, its otter-shaped body, its webbed feet, and (in males) its venom glands, the platypus would seem to have stolen bits and pieces from other mammals, not to mention reptiles and birds. No less surreal is the animal's sense of electroreception: it can locate its prey by the electrical currents generated by that prey's muscular contractions.

Sometimes the platypus will even have a pinkish coloration on its legs or tail. Might this be a theft from a flamingo? Not at all. The pink color indicates that the animal is suffering from a fungal infection known as mucormycosis. Specifically, it has one or more lesions caused by *Mucor amphibiorum*, a fungus that typically targets amphibians like green tree frogs and cane toads. Even more specifically, *M. amphibiorum* forms a yeast-like structure (formal name: mold-yeast dimorphism) in its host's connective tissue that helps it evade that host's immune system.

Fact: *Mucor* is a genus of molds (Zygomycetes) mostly found in soil, on plant surfaces, on rotting vegetables, on rodent droppings, on fruits, and -- since 1982 -- on platypuses.

The species in question isn't native to Tasmania, but if you're a fungus, you're quite happy to go non-native. All you need is someone or something to vector your spores, and off those spores go to other places and sometimes new substrates. Quite a few European and Asian fungal species, including the Death Cap (*Amanita phalloides*) and the Asian Beauty *(Radulomyces copelandii)*, have traveled to North America in the last hundred years. *M. am-*

31

*phibiorum* itself seems to have arrived in Tasmania from Australia with infected frogs, then may have bided its time in the soil as a free-living organism until an unsuspecting platypus happened to saunter along...

Note: The species might not even be native to Australia -- it could have been introduced there in 1935 from infected Hawaiian cane toads. Likewise, it's possible that both the Hawaiian and Australian strains of *M. amphibiorum* are genetically different from the Tasmanian strain.

Curiously, the fungus does not seem to affect Australian platypuses. Perhaps the cooler body temperature of Tasmanian animals, a response to the island's cooler temperatures, has encouraged its growth on a local host. Perhaps the fact that Tasmania is a typical island refuge limits that host's genetic diversity, thus making it more susceptible to the fungus. This might be the reason why another creature -- the Tasmanian devil -- is so vulnerable to the cancer known as Devil Facial Tumor Disease.

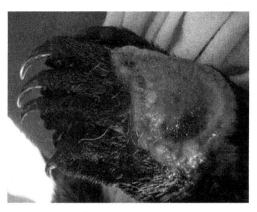

Some platypuses have pus-oozing dermal lesions over large portions of their bodies. In all likelihood, they've become spore vectors themselves, for themselves -- by itching one lesion, they've created another, and another. You can't help but feel sorry for the poor animals. At the same time, it's hard not to admire the opportunistic nature of the fungus that's causing all the trouble: an itch here, a rub there, and there's more of me, its presence seems to announce.

Speculation: In the hundred million years of its lineage, the platypus might never have suffered from mucormycosis...until this moment in time.

So we're looking at an infected platypus: will it survive, or will it succumb? If the lesions aren't severe, the animal will probably get back its health. But if those lesions become flyblown or invaded by bacteria, it might become so debilitated that it can't forage for food or maintain its body temperature. Whereupon pneumonitis, a secondary bacterial infection, or starvation could deliver the coup de grace. In certain cases, too, the lesions could spread to the animal's lungs, and if that happens, not only might the platypus bite the dust, but the fungus itself might end up in the dust, lying in wait for another platypus to come along.

I know what you're thinking: can I, a somewhat different creature from a platypus, be infected by a *Mucor* species? The answer is yes...but only if you have a badly compromised immune system. This shouldn't be surprising news. After all, we know that persons with AIDS who get a fungal infection are far more likely to die from that infection than they are from AIDS itself. Truth to tell, you're a thousand, no, ten thousand times more likely to get a Mucor infection in your bread -- i.e., "black bread mold" (*Rhizopus stolonifer*) -- than in or on your body.

But lest you develop a hostility to all *Mucorales*, let me add that certain species are utilized with each other or with bacteria to make, among other food products, tempeh, soy sauce, and miso. The last of these is a two-stage fermentation that uses strains of *Aspergillus oryzae*.

Query: Tasmania seems to specialize in extinctions. Its last aboriginal native of unmixed descent, William Lannan, died in 1869; the last Tasmanian wolf (aka, thylacine) probably died in 1936; and the Tasmanian devil is currently at risk because of Devil Facial Tumor Disease. Will the platypus be next?

With an animal that's at once secretive, nocturnal, semi-aquatic, and burrow-inhabiting, it's not easy to know what percentage of the island's population has been affected by mucormycosis. Recent (2009) studies suggest that, in the areas where the disease was originally noted, four times fewer platypuses are now suffering from it now than twenty years ago. Perhaps the platypuses in those areas, like their Australian cousins, have become immune to *M. amphibiorum.*

But don't get your hopes up yet, because the fungus now effects platypuses in parts of the island where it had been previously unknown or maybe just undetected. Thus any statement about its prevalence should conclude with a question mark. Welcome to Kingdom Fungi!

# Summit Fever
## A Mycological Horror Story

for Dick Korf

Once he arrived at Everest base camp, he immediately began his ascent. He didn't get any food from one of the Nepali take-out joints or even bother to rest his jet-lagged bones. He ignored the woman who solicited his charms for a mere 20 rupees. A man in a uniform asked to see his climbing permit, and he showed him his recent paper in *Mycologia*. That seemed to be good enough for the man.

It wasn't as if he wanted to climb Everest. He would rather be back in his lab sequencing fungi. Or giving poster presentations at conferences. But something he couldn't comprehend was driving him on.

"I'm just going out for a walk," he'd told his wife.

"You never go for a walk," she said. On her face was a worried look.

On the flight to Zurich, he'd asked himself: Why the blazes am I doing this? On the flight to New Delhi, he'd asked himself the same thing. And on the flight to Katmandu, he looked down with a certain distaste at the ice-clad mountains below the plane. After all, he didn't even like climbing a flight of stairs.

Now he was climbing something that was considerably more ambitious than even the steepest flight of stairs. Up, up, up he went, hand over hand, foot over foot. This is ridiculous, he told himself: I'm a mycologist, not a mountaineer.

Indeed, he hadn't even brought any climbing equipment with him. No pitons, no ice axe, no goggles, no carabiners, no descendeur, not even any down clothing.

A Canadian women's team passed him as he was crossing the Khumbu Icefield. "You shouldn't be climbing Everest in Birkenstocks," one of the women told him.

"They're not only the best, but also the most durable sandals in the world," he protested.

The woman gave him a look that suggested she thought he was crazy. "Go back to base camp, and get some boots with upper straps and a polyamide inner lining," she shouted at him before going on.

He knew all about bootstraps, even parsimony bootstrap consensus trees, but not about the bootstraps she was referring to. And then there was that word polyamide. He knew about polysaccharides, but not about polyamides. To say he was ignorant about climbing gear as well as climbing terminology would be a gross understatement.

But he was no less ignorant about why he was climbing this mountain. For whatever the reason, his mind kept returning to the fungal specimen that he'd received in the mail a week or so ago. Other than a note so illegible that he could only make out the phrase "Found in Asia," the specimen had arrived without any collection data. It was dramatically larger than the known species in the genus: certainly, it was larger than the species that turned ants into zombies and made them clamp onto a leaf a certain distance above the ground. But how this specimen related to his ascent of Everest (if it really did), he didn't have a clue.

Couloirs, cols, cornices, seracs -- he managed them all remarkably well for a guy who wasn't much of a field person. If only my barcoding buddies could see me now, he thought with a certain pride.

He was climbing the treacherous Lhotse Face when he lost his balance and slipped over the side. But he grabbed onto a protruding rock and somehow succeeded in pulling himself onto one of the slope's platforms. In his former life as a mild-mannered Associate Professor of Organismic Biology, he could never have performed such a feat. It almost seemed like he'd suddenly been granted superhuman powers.

36

Nightfall didn't stop him. Neither did hunger, even though he'd already eaten all the food -- two Snickers bars -- he'd brought with him. Neither did blizzards or oxygen deprivation. But he did have a terrible headache. At Camp IV, he saw the tents of a Japanese expedition. In front of one of the tents, two climbers were eating a sashimi dinner.

"Either of you guys have a Tylenol?" he asked, adding, "A generic will do." Then he thought they mightn't speak English, so he pointed to his head, rolled his eyes, and contorted his face into a grimace.

"Go down mountain," exclaimed one of the climbers. "You have embolism."

"Yes, go down now," the other one said, "or you will die."

His legs carried him away from the Japanese camp before he could say that he didn't have an embolism, and that in any event he was totally incapable of going down, only up.

Despite his footwear, he began climbing a nearly vertical pitch alongside some fixed ropes. When he reached the top of the pitch, a strong wind pelted his face with pebbles and chunks of ice. In addition to his headache, he now had an upset stomach. Damn airline food, he thought.

For perhaps the hundredth time, he tried to remember the sequence of events that had led to his becoming perhaps the world's most unlikely mountaineer. He could see his postdoc bursting into his lab. He could see the perturbed expression on the postdoc's face. He could even hear him speak these words:

"I'm fed up with analyzing just a short piece of the fungal genome, Professor. Totally, totally fed up. Only 600 nucleotide base pairs out of fucking millions!"

But he couldn't recall how he had countered this rant. In fact, he couldn't even recall his postdoc's name.

What's happening to my memory? he asked himself even as he negotiated another steep pitch. He could now see the white summit of Everest, and it was seemingly beckoning to him. The mountain called The Mother Goddess of the World by both Nepalis and Tibetans somehow felt maternal to him as well.

An hour later, he reached the so-called Death Zone. This bleak outcropping of rock was bare even of lichens. Indeed the only living things were two American climbers who'd just come down off the summit.

Here he was, a lone man in shredded Birkenstocks plunging a mushroom knife into the mountain's frozen hide, but neither of the climbers appeared to think that this was at all unusual.

One of the climbers had a face almost entirely encircled by whiskers, like a frilled ham...a frilled ham with goggly eyes. "You won't believe what we saw on the summit, man," the climber said to him.

"It was just about the weirdest thing you can imagine," the other climber said, shaking his head in disbelief.

"It was, like, even weirder than the weirdest thing you can imagine," declared the first climber. "You'll see for yourself..."

And then they continued down the mountain, muttering to themselves.

Not surprisingly, he found himself wondering what could be awaiting him on the summit. A sense of foreboding possessed him, and at the same time a sense of elation. With such contradictory emotions, he felt like he was composed of two very different selves, both of which were battling for primacy inside him. Even more peculiar, he felt as if one of these selves was not his.

He worked his way up a slippery slope, then began moving along an equally slippery ledge no more than a foot wide. He tried to imagine how many times he would bounce if he fell. But he didn't fall. Instead, he continued along the ledge until he was standing on a relatively level ice moraine.

Once again, he made an attempt to figure out why he was engaged in an activity so alien to his nature. And once again, he remembered the meeting with his postdoc.

"Yeah, I'm fed up with DNA barcoding and cladistics and all that shit," the postdoc announced. "I've decided to get a degree in wildlife management."

He tried to calm down the postdoc by handing him the "Found in Asia" specimen. "Any idea what this is?" he asked.

The postdoc held the specimen, studied it, and then shook his head. "I only know about DNA'd species, not actual ones," he lamented, handing it back.

"Maybe you could make a guess?"

"Well, it's got a stroma with lots of perithecia, so it's probably some sort of asco."

He patted his postdoc's arm paternally. "You're absolutely right," he said. "And it's really a pity that whoever collected the specimen didn't mention the substrate. Even so, I think I'm right when I say that it's an unusually large, possibly undescribed species of... of... of...?"

Of what? A week later, he could conjure up an image of the specimen, but he couldn't remember its genus. He felt like he was losing his mind.

Up ahead, he could see the gleaming white summit of Everest again, along with the cornice traverse known as the Hillary Step leading toward it. He yawned. A peculiar response, given how close he was to his goal. Even more peculiar was the fact that his mouth remained open in a yawn despite his efforts to close it.

All of a sudden he saw his wife hovering directly above a nearby scree slope. She had a resigned look on her face, and she was waving goodbye to him. After blowing him a kiss, she faded slowly away.

At the sight of his wife, or rather the sight of her apparition he attempted to shed a tear, but his tear ducts didn't respond to the message, or maybe they didn't receive it.

He was now ready for the final assault on the summit. He ascended the Hillary Step, then waded through some deep snow, and at last he was standing beside a cairn. He'd made it! Frostbitten, battered, hypoxic, and suffering from radiation burns, he'd climbed to the top of the highest mountain in the world!

Some members of a climbing group were taking photos of each other next to the same cairn. But they were also taking photos of his postdoc, who, seemingly frozen in place a few feet from the cairn, had a very large cylindrical fruiting body sticking out of his head. He recognized the fruiting body right away -- it was the same species that he and the postdoc had passed back and forth in the lab.

He didn't need to ask himself why the postdoc was here. After all, he was here for the same reason himself. The postdoc had his teeth clamped onto a pole with a red flag, a relic from a Chinese expedition. He walked over and clamped his teeth onto the same pole. It wasn't long before he felt something start to emerge from his head. His last thoughts were of the "Found in Asia" note: its illegible words doubtless said that the enclosed *Ophiocordyceps* species parasitized *Homo sapiens* rather than insects.

Within a few days, he was sporulating.

# *Notes on the Ingestion of*
# Amanita muscaria

With Tonya Haff

Boiled to remove its toxins, *Amanita muscaria* can usually be eaten with impunity. Indeed, the Japanese reputedly prefer it to *Boletus edulis*. Recently, in Santa Cruz, California, Lawrence Mill-

41

man and Tonya Haff had an experience of *A. muscaria* somewhat different from the purely culinary experience they expected to have.

Tonya cut two large *A. muscaria* fruiting bodies into 1/4" strips and placed them in two quarts of boiling water. The mushrooms were cooked for 5 minutes, then both of us sampled a few pieces. We found the flavor agreeably nutty, albeit with a slight metallic aftertaste. We browned several more slices in olive oil and found them pleasant, too. The remaining slices were breaded, then browned. Altogether, we ate almost all of the two fruiting bodies.

Twenty minutes later, both of us started to feel distinctly "off." Larry found himself staring vacantly at some mushrooms we were trying to identify. Tonya noticed that he had a frown on his face and was holding his stomach. Once we agreed that the mushroom was the culprit, we called a mycologist friend and asked him what we should do. "Take notes!" he said.

So here are the notes we took during the experience:

18:56. We ate the *A. muscarias* at 6 p.m. Tonya was initially feeling hot, but now she's feeling cold. Her sense of smell is heightened. Larry can't seem to concentrate on identifying the mushrooms we've just collected.

19:09. Tonya is slurring her words. Her pupils are dilated, and there's a lump in her throat. She finds the cedar-like odor of *Camarophyllus russocoriaceus* totally cloying. Her stomach is mildly queasy, while Larry's stomach is very queasy.

19:15. Tonya's fingers are clammy. She says her arms are unusually goosebumpy. The cedar-like odor of the waxy cap is really bothering her now. Music is bothering her as well ("Bob Dylan's driving me up a wall!"). Larry retreats to the bathroom.

19:23. Having vomited up some of the mushroom, Larry says he feels a bit better. Still, he feels buzzed and more or less out of it. He also feels quite hot.

19:27. Tonya is experiencing a heightened sense of touch.

Larry's fingers on her forehead seem to be burning a hole in her. There's an acute pain in one of her eyes, but it goes away. Larry still has the buzz, very different, he says, from the experience of being drunk or stoned. He remarks that he's glad he's not a Siberian shaman (Note: Siberian shamans eat *A. muscaria* for ritualistic purposes.)

19:38. Our "highs" seem to have stabilized. Larry is again trying to identify some of our mushrooms. Tonya says she feels almost normal, whereas Larry says he can't feel normal because he isn't normal.

19:53. Tonya is starting to feel hungry. Larry's head feels like foam.

20:00. Tonya feels dizzy when she rolls her eyes. Also sort of sleepy. Despite all odds, Larry succeeds in identifying a *Mycena*.

20:30. Tonya's feeling clumsy and poorly coordinated, but otherwise okay. Larry can't seem to dial a friend's phone number, and likewise can't close the sliding door without getting his hand stuck in it. Also, he says the mushrooms he's trying to ID are talking to him, saying "Identify us! Identify us!"

21:15. Larry's been silent for a while, listening to the mushrooms. All of a sudden, he's talkative, although he's not making much sense. "Smooth circus" -- what does that mean? "Mushrooms are people too," he says.

21:29. Both of us feel euphoric, Larry especially so -- he says he hasn't felt this good in years. We decide to go out to dinner, and since we don't think it's a good idea for either of us to drive, we appoint Tonya's roommate Mikey as our designated driver.

21:54. At a Chinese restaurant. Tonya thinks our food has a consciousness of its own as well as a texture that's "very real." She also thinks everyone in the restaurant is high, and that Larry likes Republicans, although he's earlier made it clear that he doesn't.

22:10. Larry is drinking a beer, and he says he can relate to the bottle, that the bottle can relate to him, and that the two of them are actually enjoying each other's company.

22:15. Our food feels very textured, and we seem able to communicate with each grain of rice. We also feel that we're moving fast, but that our thoughts are moving slowly. Larry keeps dropping his chopsticks. Coordination difficult for both of us.

22:30. Both of us seem to be suffering from short term memory loss. Larry feels that his critical sense, usually very much in evidence, has gone on vacation. The word "euphoria" keeps popping up in our conversation.

23:05. We leave the restaurant. We see a dead deer on the road, and Larry says the difference between a dead deer and a living one is negligible. Tonya still feels elated, but at the same time relaxed. She falls asleep around midnight without any difficulty. For the next three days, her right ring finger tingles when she hits it with her thumb, but otherwise she notices no symptoms related to *A. muscaria* ingestion. Larry has a deep sleep and wakes up the next morning feeling refreshed.

Here's what we think happened: the mushrooms were far too big for the pot in which they were boiled, with the result that only as much of the toxins were dissolved in the water as the water itself could hold. Also, we probably didn't boil the mushrooms long enough; Asians boil them for at least ten minutes. Thus our trips included a certain disarray of the senses, but not the full disarray experienced by Siberian shamans or non-shamanic contemporary trippers.

44

# Matsutake Madness

Setting out from the town of Terrace in central British Columbia, you drive northwest over washboarding seemingly calculated to destroy your transmission. You try to avert potholes so deep that they should be signposted with "Abandon Hope All Ye Who Enter." Suddenly, in the middle of an apparent nowhere, you come upon a medley of tents and tarps, converted school buses, trailers, teepees, Winnebagos, and rough-plank shanties. Welcome to Cranberry Junction (pop. 250). Or at least that's what the name on the road sign says, but nearly everyone in these parts calls this seasonal bush settlement The Zoo.

"This place has lots of animals, but they've all got two legs, and they're all here to pick mushrooms," says one of The Zoo's residents, an eroded-looking fifty-something man who goes by the name of Alberta Al.

Mushrooms -- specifically, the creamy-white to bronze-colored mushrooms called matsutakes -- are in fact The Zoo's raison d'etre. In Japan, matsutakes are symbols of fertility, wealth, and happiness. The Japanese also prize them for their subtle flavor and unique odor, described by one mycologist as "a provocative compromise between red-hots and dirty socks." Since the Japanese demand for matsutakes far exceeds the local supply, wildcat buyers descend on the rain-soaked Pacific Northwest each fall and pay pickers top dollar -- cash up front, no records kept -- for this fungal delicacy, often as much as $300 a pound in good years. In bad years, well, there's not much overhead on a teepee or plank shanty.

Not surprisingly, The Zoo is a bit like a Gold Rush town, with fortunes made, broken, or drunk away almost as fast as you can say matsutake. Its citizens are a bit like Gold Rush characters, too. They include hirsute sons and sturdy daughters of the forest, the unemployed and the unemployable, certified loonies,

45

the disenfranchised, the opportunistic, and wanderers with no fixed abode. There's a man named Wormy Pete who boasts that he hasn't had a bath in at least a year, and a toothless but otherwise attractive woman who cheerfully lowers her jeans to reveal a matsutake tattooed on each buttock.

In front of a rundown trailer sits a huge barrel of a man who calls himself Tiny. He has come all the way from Truro, Nova Scotia, more than 3,000 miles across the continent. "This is about freedom, man," he says, making a 360 degree sweep of his hand. "Freedom to roam where you like, sleep where you like, and do what you like."

After a pause, he adds, "I haven't paid a penny in taxes in five years."

His pause is not without significance; mushroom harvesting is probably Canada's most recalcitrant underground economy, so pickers tend to be somewhat reticent about speaking with outsiders, who may or may not be representatives of the law.

The Zoo has a cookhouse that offers, according to a piece of cardboard tacked to the door, "Three Coarse Meals." It has two churches, both nondenominational, and neither much bigger than one of the community's port-a-loos. It also has several illegal saloons operated by bootleggers. Supposedly, there's even a brothel.

The town is more or less deserted during the day, when pickers are roaming the steep, forested slopes of the nearby Skeena Range in search of mushroom bounty. Then, in the late afternoon or early evening, the pickers return and make a beeline for the shanties that serve as both buying depots and local hangouts. In these shanties, you might hear snatches of conversation like the following:

"Some bastard raided my patch, and all he left me with was three empty beer cans and a Snickers wrapper."

"Every mushroom I found was slushed out or full of bugs, but then I tripped on a deadfall and landed with my nose right on top of a Grade One pine (matsutake)..."

"I got a real mother lode today. Probably forty pounds of hooters (buttons) and only two or three flags (mushrooms with open caps). Just look at this beauty -- a $75 matsie!"

"...chased down a mountain by a bear, but luckily I didn't lose a single mushroom... "

Buyers sort the mushrooms into six grades, weigh them, and pass wads of bills into the hands of pickers. The thickness of the wad depends on the condition of the mushrooms, the current Asian market, and whether there's a price war going on among the buyers. It might also depend on a buyer's mood that day: if a dog bit him, the price might be lower than usual, and if his girlfriend declared her undying love, a bit higher.

Prices can shift dramatically during a twenty-four-hour period. Today's price may be almost twice yesterday's, and vice versa. There's a story about a picker who got lost in the woods for a week, and when he was found, he was suffering from severe hypothermia. Even so, he was still gripping his bag of by then rotten mushrooms. According to the story, the man's first intelligible words were, "What's...today's...price?"

Each night the closing of the buying depots is announced by a volley of gunshots. This usually occurs around nine o'clock, so the night is still young. There isn't a lot in The Zoo you can spend your money on -- no fancy restaurants, for instance, or movie theaters -- so what's a picker to do? Being somewhat thirsty by nature, he might get boozed up. Then you might see a few punches exchanged, or someone who's imbibed not wisely but too well sleeping it off in a rain puddle. And since liquor lubricates the tongue, you might also hear the occasional tall tale, like the one about the matsutake so big that it could be removed from the ground only with a winch or chainsaw.

"Despite everybody having knives and some having guns, there's not a whole lot of violence around here," observes a long-time denizen named George, who's known as the unofficial

Mayor of The Zoo. "Well, there was an incident last year when two guys got into a fight, and one ended up beating the other so badly that he nearly killed him. But they were fighting over a woman, not mushrooms. Somehow I think they got their priorities mixed up."

Increasingly frigid temperatures and even moderate snowfall would not deter stalwarts like George, Alberta Al, Tiny, or a woman who calls herself The Iron Maiden, but frost and snow do deter matsutakes. So it is that when the weather turns wintry, the pickers pull up stakes and either go home or head south along the mushroom trail, to places like Bella Coola and Boston Bar in British Columbia, and then later in the season to Washington and Oregon.

Whereupon The Zoo, bereft of its nomadic menagerie, once again becomes Cranberry Junction, a mere potholed crossroads in the back of the Great Northern Beyond.

# A Home in the Arctic

East Greenland is not to be confused with West Greenland. The latter has a large percentage of the island's population, forests of fifteen foot high trees, and a region commonly referred to as The Banana Coast even before the assaults of global warming. East Greenland, on the other hand, is wind-blasted, ice-clogged, and far more obviously Arctic in character.

Not surprisingly, a number of wood-inhabiting fungi -- mostly corticioid species that occur on finger-thick trunks and branches -- have been found in West Greenland, especially in its valleys. But not a single wood-inhabiting basidiomycete has ever been documented in East Greenland. Ascomycetes such as *Rosellinia* and *Diatrypella* species, yes; but no basidios. This is also not surprising, given the absence of sufficiently large woody substrates.

In the summer of 2012, I visited the East Greenland village of Tasiilaq (formerly Angmagssalik), and you can guess one of my goals: to find a polypore or crust fungus. To that end, I spent a considerable amount of time examining dwarf birches and dwarf willows (the only trees in East Greenland are dwarves) within five or so miles of the village...and found nothing. There were plenty of fleshy fungi like *Russulas, Inocybes,* and *Amanitas,* but not a single wood inhabitor.

At one point, I indicated my interest in fungi to the Danish curator of the Tasiilaq Museum, and he took me to an old turf house situated just below the Museum. It was the sort of dwelling that East Greenlanders, otherwise known as Tunumiut, would have used for a winter abode until well into the 20th century. Traditionally, such houses would have been entered through a long, low passageway, but nowadays no one seems to enjoy crawling, so the house had been provided with a regular door.

Inside the structure, the curator shined his flashlight on what looked like a white crust fungus growing along the beam above the door. It had appeared not long after the village snow plough had dumped a large amount of snow on top of the house, he said. Could a large amount of melting snow have created the right conditions for the fungus? he asked me. Maybe, I replied, using one of my favorite mycological terms.

Or perhaps I should have used another of my favorite mycological terms: probably. For in 2009 I had investigated wood-rot fungi in several buildings in the Arctic archipelago of Svalbard, and what usually inspired these fungi to produce fruiting bodies was the fact that the inside of the building in question had somehow become unusually wet.

I collected a piece of the white entity and, once I returned home, I looked at it under the microscope. I saw hyphae and all sorts of cystidia, but no spores. Then I tried unsuccessfully to culture it. At last I gave a sample to my friend Bob Blanchette, a mycologist at the University of Minnesota. Bob extracted DNA directly from the tissue of my sample. The sequencing result: a 99% match with the crust fungus *Peniophorella* (=*Hyphoderma*) *praetermissa*.

This not uncommon species (probably a species complex) is a widely spread generalist in the northern hemisphere. It has been recorded on gray willow (*Salix glauca*) from several localities in West Greenland, so it seemed possible that some of its spores had traveled east across the Ice Cap and gotten into the beams of the turf house. Or maybe someone from West Greenland had those spores on his person and visited the turf house. Or maybe a visitor from northern Europe had wandered into the turf house. I had a more intriguing explanation for the presence of the fungus in the house, however.

*Peniophorella praetermissa* is often found in or on Siberian drift logs. The logs are originally infected by its spores or mycelium in Siberia itself, then they end up in one of the region's great rivers -- the Lena, the Yenisei, and the Ob. That river transports them to the seas north of Siberia, where -- usually frozen in ice -- they tend to be shuffled around the Arctic by the clockwise Beaufort Gyre or the more erratic Transpolar Drift. While many of these logs continue their journey to northern Canada and Alaska, some of them are taken down the coast of East Greenland by the strong East Greenland Current. Their journey from Siberia to a beach in East Greenland might take ten years, maybe longer.

Now let's imagine this scenario: a hundred or so years ago, an East Greenlandic man is constructing a turf house for his family's overwintering. Wandering the shore near Tasiilaq, he finds an appropriately-sized drift log and decides to use it for some of the beams in that house, thus providing that log's resident fungus with a different habitat. The fungus may have infected the core of the wood, but it doesn't produce a fruiting body until shortly after a certain snow plough happens to come along...

You might think that a long Arctic journey like the one I've just described would be the kiss of death for a fungus. Not at all. For fungi are not only robust, but they can also be extremely long-lived. To cite an example: researchers from Texas A&M University have recently found in ocean sediments fungi that could be as much as 100 million years old. The researchers were able to culture those fungi, which turned out to be related to present-day *Penicillium* species. By comparison, ten or so years of being trundled about in frigid seas (conifers are more buoyant, deciduous logs less buoyant) and even as long as several hundred years of resting on a frigid beach, like some logs on the Arctic island of Jan Mayen have done, are a mere blip in time.

Such was my hypothesis. As it happens, it turned out to be completely wrong. For not long after I concocted it, I received an email from Ole Jensen, the former curator of the Tasiilaq Museum, informing me that the turf house in question was a relatively recent replica. Ole added that the wood used to construct the house had spent no time whatsoever in Arctic seas. Rather, it had arrived by ship from Denmark. I consoled myself with the fact that fungi are highly egalitarian: a Danish log, for a fungus, is just as charismatic a substrate as a Siberian drift log, and a replica turf hut is no different from a genuine one.

If a Danish mycelium produces a fruiting body in East Greenland, then that fruiting body should probably be considered a Danish species. Yet if the *P. praetermissa* mycelium remains in the replica turf house, and if that mycelium decides to produce another fruiting body, and if the next fruiting body produces spores, and if some of those spores insinuate themselves into the wood of a non-replica house in Tasiilaq, then an East Greenlander might have the privilege of documenting the first native wood-inhabiting basidiomycete in this remote part of the Arctic.

# Concerning a Mysterious Asian Beauty

With J. Ginns

In mid-November 2009, one of us (LM) found a quite re-markable tooth fungus on a large red maple (*Acer rubrum*) log at Bradley Palmer State Park in Ipswich, Massachusetts.

The fruiting body was resupinate (flat on the log's surface

and lacking a pileus), and its white to cream-colored spines were both densely crowded and unusually long (8 to 12 mm). Indi-vidual fruit bodies of several decimeters in length grew out of the cracks and interstices in the log's bark, presumably using this feature of the substrate for both moisture and insulation.

Having never encountered such a fungus before, LM collect-ed a sample specimen and brought it home to identify. Finding no match for it either macroscopically or microscopically, he sent the sample to JG, who, after a lot of searching and head scratch-ing, concluded that the beautiful, spiny fungus had the scien-tific name *Radulomyces copelandii* (Pat. Hjortstam & Spooner). A surprising conclusion, because this fungus previously had been found only in Asia.

From January 2010 to March 2010, LM found fruitings of *R. copelandii* on northern red oak (*Quercus rubra*), white oak (*Q. alba*), and beech (*Fagus grandifolia*) in three other eastern Massachusetts localities: in Concord, near Walden Pond; in Lincoln, near Mt. Misery; and in Sharon, at Moose Hill Audubon Sanctuary. He figured that the reason the Asian Beauty had not been collected earlier was that it fruited in the winter, a time when very few mycologists venture into the field. He suspected that the species was unusually cold tolerant, as he'd found it in freezing or sub-freezing temperatures with snow on the ground. Also, each time he'd brought home a sample for microscopic study, he'd found it eagerly sporulating. This caused him to wonder whether *R. copelandii* possessed some kind of unusual glyco-protein or some other chemical that allows it to turn carbohydrates into sugars with extreme alacrity. None of the admittedly few articles on the species at Harvard University's Farlow Herbarium provided any mention of its chemicals, unusual or not.

But this paper concerns a *mysterious* Asian Beauty, not simply an Asian Beauty with a preference for cold weather, so here the story gets more complicated. During the fall of 2010, LM found *R. copelandii* on almost every collecting trip he made in eastern Massachusetts, including one urban locale -- Fresh Pond in Cambridge. As before, it was fruiting on a large hardwood log, in the cracks and interstices of the bark. Thus it would appear that the species doesn't fruit only in the winter, and likewise that it has found a very comfortable niche as a saprobe in eastern Massachusetts. To date, LM has not found *R. copelandii* beyond a 35 mile radius of Boston, but he suspects that will change in the not too distant future. (Note: It did change -- LM recently found a specimen at Wachusett Meadow Wildlife Sanctuary in central Massachusetts).

It surprised us that a fungus known only from eastern Asia (China, Japan, Korea, the Philippines, and to the Russian Far

East) would be found not just once but several times in eastern North America. We sought confirmation that our Asian Beauty was R. *copelandii* by asking Dr. Karen Nakasone, who has studied species in this and allied genera, for her opinion. She confirmed our identification, adding that this was the first collection of R. *copelandii* in the Western Hemisphere.

Most readers will not have heard of *Radulomyces*, but over 20 species have been placed in the genus. Several studies have discussed the circumscription of this genus and whether R. *copelandii* might be better placed in another genus.

To determine which species were closely related to R. *copelandii*, part of specimen # 11837 was sent to Drs. Ellen and Karl-Henrik Larsson, who sequenced the full nuclear ribosomal ITS region and about 1500 basepairs of the adjacent end of the LSY region. Their results showed R. *copelandii* to be in a well defined clade with R. *confluens* (type species of the genus), R. *molaris*, and R. *rickii*.

This species is generally included in a group called crust fungi. Identification of many crusts requires the examination of their microscopic features such as basidiospores, cystidia, and hyphae. And that was how we named the collections R. *copelandii*. However, it is relatively easy to identify R. *copelandii* without reference to a microscope because of its long spines and large, pale yellowish fruiting bodies.

The most obvious question is: how did the Asian Beauty reach eastern Massachusetts? LM's initial collection (not to mention five subsequent collections and numerous "sightings") came from Bradley Palmer State Park, part of the former 10,000 acre estate of a wealthy attorney named Bradley Palmer (1864-1948). An avid gardener and horticulturist, Mr. Palmer imported many plants from Scotland because he thought the Scottish climate was similar to New England's. On at least one occasion, he brought in plants from Asia -- a whole freight car of azaleas, rhododendrons, and laurel.

Could the mycelium of *R. copelandii* have somehow hitched a ride with these acid-loving members of the heath family? Perhaps, but almost a hundred years separates this putative introduction from LM's discovery of a fruiting body. *Radulomyces copelandii* would not appear to be a slow-working pathogen like *Grifola frondosa* or *Laetiporus sulphureus*, so it would not require nearly such a lengthy time to complete its cycle.

A related question: assuming the Asian Beauty didn't arrive via the enterprise of Mr. Palmer, when and how did it arrive? A thorough search of the literature on tooth fungi at Harvard's Farlow Herbarium turned up no reference to any earlier North American collection or, indeed, any description of a species that might have been *R. copelandii* in an earlier taxonomic guise. Nor did a search of the inventories from amateur and regional forays turn up an even remotely similar species. Of course, such searches don't prove that *R. copelandii* hadn't fruited before 2009, especially if fruitings typically occurred in the winter. Yet the numerous collections and/or sightings from the late summer through the fall of 2010 indicates that the species also fruits during the so-called mushroom season, when it would be hard to overlook.

It might be argued that the Asian Beauty has a stubborn or desultory mycelium, one that produces a fruiting body only once in a great while. Certainly, this is true of some species mistakenly listed as rare. However, a mycelium in a deteriorating woody substrate has a life expectancy for only as long as that substrate can provide it with nutrients. The absence of any collection in the last thirty years would seem to indicate that *R. copelandii* is a relatively recent arrival in eastern Massachusetts. Exactly how recent is probably impossible to ascertain at this point.

Another question: might the fact that the Asian Beauty has established a seemingly comfortable niche in eastern Massachusetts have negative consequences? As a saprobe, it might be replacing or at least nudging aside native polypores as well as other crust fungi. Such species, in addition to being wood recyclers, would have a complex network of relationships with organisms like birds, insects, microbes, and other fungi. If the Asian Beauty was interfering with these relationships, it might be described as an invasive. Or if not an invasive, at least a takeover species, a fact evidenced by the dramatically increased number of fruitings of 2010. (Note: since 2010, fruitings have decreased somewhat.)

We consider this paper by its very nature to be inconclusive. In writing it, we hope: to alert both mycologists and the public to a significant new species in eastern Massachusetts; to inspire further studies of this species' range and preferred habitats; and to encourage an investigation into whether the effect of *R. cope-landii* on local ecosystems is good, bad, or indifferent.

See Appendix I for more information on *Radulomyces cope-landii*.

# In Search of an Extinct Polypore

for Leif Ryvarden

This story begins with a statement of religious devotion: both fellow mycologist Bill Neill and I were (and still are) avid readers of the Bible, by which I mean the two capacious volumes of *North American Polypores* by Leif Ryvarden and the late Robert Gilbertson. We would note odd, obscure, or rare species on its pages, and then venture into the field in search of them. Thus it's not surprising that we developed an interest, no, an obsession with finding *Echinodontium ballouii*, a species that hadn't been sighted since 1909. Indeed, the Bible referred to it as being "possibly extinct."

Before I describe our adventures in the field, I should mention that it's rather difficult to determine whether or not a fungal entity is extinct. For one thing, that entity's mycelium might be laggard, slothful, or downright recalcitrant about producing a fruiting body. For another, it's a lot easier to overlook a fungus than it is to overlook (for example) a celebrity woodpecker. A case in point: *Bridgeoporus nobilissimus*, a polypore that boasts the largest fruiting body in the world, wasn't discovered until as recently as 1943.

If not extinct, *E. ballouii* was at least extremely rare. It grew only on Atlantic White Cedar (*Chamaecyparis thyoides*), a tree highly susceptible to chloride, elevated nitrogen concentrations, and changes in hydrology. What's more, it grew only on very old trees, which were themselves rare in the northeastern part of the U. S. (and almost non-existent elsewhere) due to the extensive use of their rot-resistant wood in shipbuilding. William Hosea Ballou, the remarkably amateur paleontologist and mycologist who first found *E. ballouii*, called his eponymous species "deadly." This statement was on the same footing with his belief that

58

the stegosaurus could fly. What was deadly were Ballou's fellow hominids, who were cutting down Atlantic White Cedars with reckless abandon.

Atlantic White Cedars are swamp inhabitors, so if you want to find a fungus growing on them, you have to deal with muck, mosquitoes, and pools of water camouflaged by moss, not to mention pools of uncamouflaged water. That's why the optimal foraging season is the winter, and also why Bill and I were constantly hoping for snow. For snow meant we could put on our primary mycological appurtenance, snowshoes, and thus wander around the swamp of our choice with relative ease.

On our initial forays, we snowshoed around Ponkapoag, a relict Atlantic White Cedar swamp south of Boston; we snowshoed around another relict swamp at Mashpee in Cape Cod; and we made a snowshoe trek through another swamp north of Manchester, New Hampshire. But we didn't find any specimens of *E. ballouii*. There were hardly any old growth trees in any of the aforementioned swamps, either.

On a cold afternoon in early March, 2006, we found ourselves in southern New Hampshire. We had already visited several Atlantic White Cedar swamps earlier in the day, and we were thinking of heading back to Boston and perhaps finding a tavern where we could raise a non-celebratory pint or two. But something seemed to compel us to visit one last swamp before giving up. For security reasons, I won't reveal the location of this swamp. Let's just say that it was quite a distance from the nearest strip mall, Golden Arches, or condo development.

As soon as we snowshoed into the swamp, we began seeing old growth trees, and we performed the maneuver that we invariably performed in an Atlantic White Cedar swamp -- we raised our binoculars to our eyes. For *E. ballouii* typically grows high in the crown of its substrate, a fruiting habit that makes binoculars a necessity. We also began seeing cankers of *Gymnosporangium biseptatum* and *G. clavipes*. Another good sign. For *Gymnosporangium*

59

is a possible indicator species for *E. ballouii*. Appearing in the final stages of wood decay, the latter species needs the former to weaken a tree's defenses or an aggressive primary decayer before it can begin dinner itself. (Species that arrive late for dinner are not uncommon among wood inhabitors -- their numbers include *Serpula himantoides*, *Antrodia crassa*, *Coltriciella dependens*, and *Diplomitoporus lenis*, among others.)

So here's the scene: a failing light; intermittent snowfall; an eerie mist hovering two or three feet above the ground; and a raven that seemed to be following us through the swamp, making the occasional expostulating croak. All of a sudden Bill pointed to a blackened mass on the trunk of a tree and suggested that it might be the object of our quest, albeit in a posthumous state.

I was skeptical. Then we walked in opposite directions around the same tree, and on the other side, at eye level, we became perhaps the first individuals to see an actual specimen of *E. ballouii* in the field in almost a century. The specimen in question had a moss-ridden, faintly zonate pileus and a pinkish toothlike hymenium. This not necessarily dramatic description doesn't mean that we didn't think our discovery was dramatic. Truth to tell, it was beyond dramatic. We were speechless, and that permitted the fungus itself to take the floor: extinction, it informed us, doesn't need to be forever.

In the next fifteen or twenty minutes, we found half a dozen more specimens, each on a branch stub or at the axis where a branch joined the trunk. We took notes, measured specimens (average pileus length: 5 1/2 cm), GPS'd sites, and -- having lost our speechlessness -- yelled enthusiastically every time we found a new specimen. In the end, we collected a single specimen -- actually, two specimens: my camera lens accidentally knocked a second one from its substrate while I was taking a photo -- and snowshoed back to the car in, by now, total darkness.

When I got home, I put a slice from my specimen under my microscope and saw that it was sporulating...a not unusual activity in the winter for a perennial polypore. I compared the spores with the description in *North American Polypores*. They were ellipsoid, finely echinulate, and strongly amyloid, as indicated by the book's description, but they were also slightly smaller -- 5.5-7.0 by 3.8-5.8 microns to the book's 7-8 by 4-6 microns.

Bill took his specimen to Manfred Binder at Clark University to sequence. The best match comparing sequences turned out to be *Echinodontium ryvardenii* (99%), a species found only in ancient creeping juniper forests on the Italian island of Sardinia. Both *E. ballouii* and *E. ryvardenii* were sufficiently different from the type species, *Echinodontium tinctorium*, that they probably belong in another genus, perhaps, according to Swedish mycologist K.

H. Larssen, *Laurilia*. Turnabout is fair play: a 1964 monograph on *Echinodontium* (Gross, H., *Mycopathology*, vol. 24, xi, Fasc. 1) argued that *Laurilia* should be placed in *Echinodontium*.

But the story doesn't end yet. With Bill otherwise engaged, I continued to investigate Atlantic White Cedar swamps in the Northeast. One likely candidate, a swamp on Naushon Island off Cape Cod, hadn't been logged since the 1820s; some of its trees exceeded 75 cm in diameter. But a winter visit to Naushon yielded no new specimens of *E. ballouii*, not even posthumous ones. The species seemed to be restricted to one site; and though several other swamps had appropriately-sized trees, no spore corridor seemed to connect these swamps with that one site.

Several winters later, I decided to get some good pictures of *E. ballouii*, so I returned to the New Hampshire swamp with photographer-entomologist Tom Murray. Despite the fact that I had GPS coordinates, we succeeded in getting lost and ended up in a very different part of the swamp. No matter. I still raised my binoculars to my eyes and almost immediately saw what looked like a resupinate specimen of *E. ballouii* thirty or so feet above my head. Then Tom shouted. I snowshoed over to where he was standing and pointing. On the slender trunk of what looked like a young Atlantic White Cedar, there were five effused fruiting bodies. Each was exhibiting its pinkish hymenium to us, as if to say, Aren't I sexy?

As Tom was photographing the specimens, I contemplated this new discovery. *E. ballouii* reputedly grows only on old growth trees, and likewise only on a tree that has already been weakened or subjected to a certain amount of decay. Had the species been so little studied that information about its substrate was scanty? Perhaps the "young tree" was older than it looked. After all, some of the Atlantic White Cedars in the Marconi Swamp on Cape Cod were quite old despite their relatively youthful appearance. Or perhaps *E. ballouii* had adapted to its near-extinct status by becoming more liberal about the age of its substrates...

One thing was certain, however: while there might not have been a spore corridor between this swamp and other Atlantic White Cedar swamps in the Northeast, there was a seemingly healthy spore corridor between two distant parts of this particular swamp.

On the way out of the swamp, we managed to get lost again. *Mea culpa!* As the guide, I was constantly looking up at the crowns of trees rather than where I should have been looking, at the ground and our snowshoe prints on it. We headed in one direction, then another, and then yet another. At one point, we found ourselves crossing a frozen river. Or I should say a mostly frozen river. One ill-considered step would have meant a frigid dunking, hypothermia, or possibly worse, so we proceeded very cautiously, inching our way across. Eventually, by some peculiar quirk, we ended up back at the car. We were exhausted, utterly exhausted, but why shouldn't field mycology be an exhausting experience on occasion?

The story doesn't end here, either. That's because no mycological story has a real ending. Since fungi delight in trumping our speculations about them, my remark about the absence of an extended spore corridor might be pure bunk. Even as I write these words, there might be an *E. ballouii* mycelium lurking in an old or maybe not-so-old Atlantic White Cedar somewhere in the Northeast, lurking and waiting, holding its fruiting bodies in reserve for just the right moment.

# A Scatological Tale

for Rex Passion

Last February I went for a hike in the woods outside Boston with several friends. There was a cold wind blowing from the east, and the temperature was no higher than 25°F. At one point, one of my friends noticed some deer dung, so I squatted down and put a few boluses of it in my collecting vial.

"I thought you were a mycologist, not a scatologist," an-oth-er of my friends remarked.

"Sometimes they're the same thing," I replied.

When I got home, I incubated the dung in a moist petri dish. Within a few days, there was a large fruiting of *Pilobolus* growing on the dung. Each little fruiting body seemed to epitomize, in the words of mycologist Harold Brodey, "the glass-blowers art." After a while, the bladder-like sporangia burst, and spores deco-rated the inside of the petri dish.

The following week, several small yellowish cup fungi with hairs on their margins appeared on the dung. Ah, I thought, *La-siobolus ciliatus*. If *Pilobolus* is an example of the glass-blowers art, *L. ciliatus* is an example of a highly talented miniature sculptor's.

In the next few days, the dung hosted a colony of *Ascobolus*, possibly *A. furfuracea*. Under the microscope, they boasted quite large asci and bright purple spores -- an esthetic treat!

Soon I noticed a batch of small fuzzy fruiting bodies on the dung. As if by magic, they developed longish stipes, and I knew that I had what might be called a shitload of *Coprinus*. None of the delicate caps was more than a few millimeters in diameter, but this did not prevent them from liquefying into a black inky goo when their time to sporulate arrived.

Still later I had a second fruiting of *Pilobilus*, and then more *Coprinus*. In fact, the *Coprinus* mycelium aggressively takes over its substrate, so henceforth the only fungal entity that grew on the dung was more *Coprinus*. And yet more *Coprinus*.

The moral of this little tale is simple: if you want to make a mycologically-minded person happy, give him shit.

# Spring Foraging in Slovakia

During a recent mycological trip to Slovakia, the southern part of the former Czechoslovakia, I didn't hear any of the dour-faced binomial bashing that I so often hear in my own country. Instead, I heard remarks like the following:

"We need to be drinking when we're identifying fungi. Otherwise, how could we come up with any new species?"

The speaker of these words was Ivona Kautmanova, an expert mycologist based in Bratislava, the country's capital. We were drinking an apricot schnapps and looking at what turned out to be *Daedaleopsis tricolor*. It wasn't the schnapps that gave us this name, however. *D. tricolor* is a European species that differs from the common American species *D. confragosa* in being more lamellate and having a pileus that alternates bands of color, with one of those colors often a deep red.

During the day, we'd been looking for another lamellate poly-pore, *Lenzites warnieri*. This species fruits in the fall, but doesn't sporulate until the spring. In Slovakia, it has been found only once, on a willow tree growing on the Danube floodplain. On that floodplain, I'd examined every willow in sight, occasionally sinking several inches into riparian muck, but no *Lenzites*.

*L. warnieri* is on the Red List of Slovakian fungi, and while Ivona and I didn't find it, we did find another Red Listed species, *Myriostoma coliforme*. This odd earthstar has pore mouths all over its exoperidium…hence its genus name ("*Myriostoma*" means "many mouths"). There were only a few localities in the country where it had been documented.

A word about the Red Listing of fungi: Although a project is in the works to get threatened fungi Red Listed globally, rare or uncommon fungi are now only protected by country. For example, 35% of all fungi have been placed on Germany's Red List, and several hundred species have been similarly designated in Slovakia. In the U.S., however, only two lichens and one fungal species have been Red Listed. Call it zoocentricism, call it mycophobia, or call it the American Way. Perhaps call it a melange of all three...

This was early April, a period when unusual ascomycetes fruit in Slovakia, so the next day I went to a piney sand plain northeast of Bratislava with Ivona, her husband Vaclav, and an ascomycete specialist named Milan. Milan had found several species at this site that hadn't been found elsewhere in Slovakia.

Almost as soon as we got out of the car, I noticed that lots of trees had been recently cut. Ivona told me that such cutting was illegal. When I asked her why the forestry people didn't punish the felons, she told me that the forestry people were the felons.

"Maybe all this cutting will aid biodiversity," I said, trying to look on the bright side. After all, there are more species of fungi in a disturbed forest than in a primary forest.

"Ah, biodiversity," Milan remarked. "You Americans love it so much that you would even bring *Ebola* into your country just to improve the biodiversity."

This jocular observation raised an as-yet unanswered question about the Red Listing of fungi: if a species is at once uncommon and a serious pathogen, should it be Red Listed? Or might we assume that an uncommon species doesn't do much damage precisely because it's uncommon?

Soon I began finding *Discinas* everywhere. Maybe they were *D. perlata*, but maybe they were not — European species are not always the same as their North American lookalikes, and visa versa.

Vaclav was an entomologist, and like quite a few entomologists of my acquaintance, he had exceptionally sharp eyes. He pointed to something that I didn't see. He pointed again, and I didn't see it again. At last he touched the specimen he was pointing at, and I saw a fruiting body of *Sclerotina* (=*Dumantina*) *tuberosa*.

The common name of this monotypic discomycete, Anemone Cup, indicates its substrate — the black sclerotia of anemones. Specimens typically have a thin meandering stipe that's well nigh invisible...except to the harrowed sclerotia and individuals like Vaclav.

We didn't find any fleshy fungi, but my companions did tell me about one, *Tylopilus felleus* (aka, the Bitter Bolete), that made an excellent libation when dried and put into vodka for several weeks. They said that the vodka becomes slightly, but not unpleasantly bitter. I made a point to make this drink later in the year, when *T. felleus* fruits with reckless abandon in my neck of the woods.

For years, I'd been looking for the discomycete *Plectania melastoma*. Looked in North America, in Europe, in Iceland, but I'd never found it. We were studying the piney debris at the edge

of the forest when I suddenly shouted: "Holy shit!" For directly front of me was a large cluster of *P. melastoma*. The spe-cies
is unmistakable — it has a blackish-brown cup encrusted with
orangish-red granules and a slightly toothed margin.

Here I should add that *P. melastoma* is another species on
the Slovakian fungal Red List, and that this particular locale —
according to Milan — was the only one in the country where it
had been documented. In being Red Listed, it can't be collected
without a permit.

"What would happen to someone who collected it without a
permit?" I asked Ivona.

"They would be fined 100 Euros," she said. Then she asked
me about the penalty for collecting Red Listed fungi in my country.

There would be no penalty, I told her, because there's no Red
Listing…yet.

I added that if, on the other hand, a person was caught with
a collection basket full of spotted owls, he/she would be penal-
ized, perhaps severely.

Toward the end of the day, a man whose rigging was a bit
disheveled joined us. He turned out to be a local farmer. When
he learned that we were mycologists, he removed a specimen
from his pocket and showed it to us. "Could you look at this
*huba* [mushroom]?" he said. "I found it recently, and I think it's
*Coltricia perennis*."

We looked at the specimen. It was indeed a *Coltricia perennis*.

That evening we celebrated a successful foray with the usual
schnapps.

Truth to tell, I did not come up with a new name for anything we had collected. Rather, I raised my glass and toasted Slovakia, its spring ascos, and its mycologically aware farmers, not
to mention its Red Listing of rare fungi.

# Foraging with Headhunters

Some years ago an explorer friend just back from Borneo told me that the most knowledgeable mycophiles he'd encountered on the island were a Native people, the Iban. I knew the Iban had a reputation for plucking off human heads, but I didn't know that they also plucked mushrooms, so in February of 2001, finding myself in Sarawak (the Malaysian part of Borneo), I decided to investigate my friend's claim.

From Kuching, Sarawak's capital, I took a motorized, albeit minimally-horsepowered dugout canoe into the island's interior. This was the rainy season, so it was raining much of the time; and when it wasn't raining, the humidity was so thick that I could barely distinguish it from rain. At one point Bakhri, my half-Iban, half Malay guide, handed me a dainty Japanese umbrella, and a particularly violent downpour soon blasted a gaping hole in it. Needless to say, I got wet on the trip. Very wet.

After what seemed like an eternity, we arrived at our destination, the Iban longhouse of Nanga Ghokan. This structure was true to its name, since it stretched for perhaps three hundred feet along the Permanak River. As we walked up to it, I noticed an encrusting patch of *Coniophora* on one of the longhouse's stilts.

Ah, I thought to myself, the wet rot of home, and felt strangely comforted.

An hour or so later, I was seated on a mat next to the chief. On the other side of me was the local *manang* (shaman), a man whose circuitry of blue-black tattoos made him resemble a giant thumbprint. And dangling from the rafters directly above me was a rattan bag of skulls belonging to former members of the Japanese Imperial Army: they dated back to World War II and were, Bakhri assured me, the last heads this particular group of Iban had taken.

I was wearing a "Shiitake Happens" T-shirt, and the chief

wanted to know what the words meant; through Bakhri, I explained them to him, and he clapped his hands in delight, remarking that he hadn't heard anything so funny in years.

When dinner was announced. Bakhri told me that he had mentioned my interest in *kulat* (mushrooms) to our hosts, and now they had a treat for me. The treat turned out to be our meal's entrée -- a plate of glutinous rice with a liberal topping of *Schizophyllum commune*, the so-called Split Gill.

"*Kulat dadapr*," said Bakhri. "Favorite *kulat* of Iban."

All eyes were on me as I stuck a couple of *Schizophyllums* into my mouth, chewed, and then nodded my head in approval. In truth, the S. *commune* had the consistency of leather and a flavor to match. That it was considered a local delicacy (so, too, were monkey eyes) proved that there is no disputing matters of taste.

The next day was relatively dry. and a group of us went for a mushroom foray behind the longhouse. Fittingly, the *manang* was our foray leader. Almost immediately he pointed to a branch covered with *Auricularia* and said something in Iban.

Bakhri translated his words as follows: "He say that when a child doesn't listen to advice, his parents tell him he has ears like this *kulat*."

The *manang* now pointed to several *Calostomas* that had bright yellow spore cases and stalks that were even more brightly yellow.

Bakhri again translated his words: "If someone has a fever, *manang* will make a tea out of this *kulat*, and then the fever will go away."

"What's the name for it?" 1 said.

"*Mata babi*. Eye of pig. You see, it looks like eye of wild pig. Also, this" -- he touched a *Calostoma's* gelatinous stalk -- "looks like the stuffing [nerves] behind wild pig's eye."

Before long, we found ourselves climbing a steep hill. At one point, I saw a specimen of *Phaeotrametes decipiens* on a dead branch. According to mycologist Leif Ryvarden, this tropical polypore is not related to any other genus, and thus might in fact be a living fossil. The *manang* did not know about polypore taxonomy, but he did say that the Iban sometimes used a piece of *P. decipiens* as a mushroom-flavored chewing gum.

Just after we reached the crest of the hill, a python slithered across the trail and disappeared into the jungle. Two of our foragers, a pair of teenage boys, charged off after it. They returned a short while later with the now dead seven foot reptile mounted on their shoulders. Deep knife gashes made it look even more reticulated than it already was.

"What are they going to do with that snake?" I asked Bakhri.

"Eat it," he replied, giving me a look that seemed to say, What else would you do with a dead python?

The two boys, joined by a third lad, carried the python back to the longhouse. Meanwhile, our foray continued. I saw dozens of *Russula, Crepidotus, Marasmius, Coprinus,* and brightly-colored *Hygrocybe* species. For probably half of them, the *manang* seemed to have a name. What, I asked him, was the first thing he considered when trying to identify a *kulat*?

Being a good mycologist, he uttered the word *penumboh*, which Bakhri translated as "the place where something grows" -- i.e., the substrate. The *manang* went on to say that *Kulat engkabang*, a toxic mushroom (from his description, this seemed to be a species of *Russula*), grew primarily under old illipe-nut trees, whereas its edible lookalike, *Kulat muyong tunggal*, usually occurred in the vicinity of anthills.

"The Iban used to eat *Kulat muyong tunggal* at headhunting feasts," he said. "It is a very special mushroom."

Now it was Bakhri's turn to pose a question. He asked the *manang* whether there was any *kulat* in these parts that could kill a person.

"*Kulat bari*," the *manang* said without hesitation. He described a large greenish mushroom with a ring and basal bulb, possibly *Amanita phalloides*. To the best of his knowledge, only two Iban had died from eating *K. baris*, and both had died before his time. He implied that his people were far too savvy to mistake a deadly mushroom for an edible one, although he did know of several cases where people from his longhouse had gotten quite sick from eating another, less deadly mushroom, *Kulat ipoh*. This latter mushroom presumably derives its name from the poisonous latex of the ipoh tree (*Antiaris toxiaria*). From what I could gather, it was another species of *Russula*, one whose toxins, whatever they were, seemed quite atypical for the genus.

At this point, the *manang* quoted a saying: *Indu bebari enda netu, enda tan dempa kulat tu* (If flies are not attracted to it, a mushroom isn't edible). This clearly wasn't true, he told me, for he had often seen flies buzzing around specimens of *Kulat ipoh*. I cited a similarly dangerous folk belief from my own neck of the woods -- that a toxic mushroom will turn a silver coin or silver spoon black.

We were now walking along a stream that seemed to consist entirely of oxbows. Near its bank was *Mimosa pudica*, the so-called sensitive plant, and the *manang* grabbed several handfuls of its fernlike leaves. Was he going to use them as a diuretic? Not at all. There was a man in the longhouse whose wife had left him, and the man wanted her back. So he, the *manang*, would feed the wife a tea made from the leaves of this evergreen shrub.

There was nothing better for regaining the affections of a woman, he solemnly informed me.

Not far from the mimosa was a trooping of *Agaricus campestris* or, more probably, a tropical variant of it. "What do you call this *kulat*?" I asked the *manang*.

He shook his head and said that the Iban did not have names for certain toxic mushrooms, like, for instance, this one. When 1 indicated that it was one of the most popular edibles in America, he remarked, in effect, that Americans must have cast-iron stomachs.

A short while later, we wandered over to the much-decayed log of a sepetir tree (*Sindora corrocea*) on which grew a large fruiting of a *Xylaria* species. The *manang* indicated that the Iban regard this elongated ascomycete, which they call *Kulat tusu habi* (Sow's Nipple Fungus), as a good edible. Indeed, one of the women in our group had already begun removing the *Xylarias* from the log for later consumption.

Once again I was struck by the fact that one culture's meat is another culture's, if not poison, at least flagrant inedible.

The foray was almost over when I heard shrieks and giggling from the women in our group. They were pointing to a fresh fruiting of stinkhorns on the edge of the communal pepper garden.

The *manang* explained their reaction as follows:

The Iban think the stinkhorn in question, *Dictyophora indusi-ata*, is the penis of a ghost, hence its name *Kulat butoh anturaya* (Ghost Penis Fungus). More precisely, they think it's the penis of a warrior whose head was lopped off in battle. If you happen to eat or even pick the mushroom, the warrior will rise from the ground and chase after you. He will not give up until he has cut off your own head with his *parang* (headhunting sword).

"Have you ever seen one of these ghostly warriors?" I inquired.

"Yes," replied the *manang*. laughing, "but only after drinking too much rice wine..."

That evening we had roasted python for dinner. Since I seemed to have liked *Schizophyllum* so much the previous night, it was served once again, this time as a garnish for the python. And once again I found it more or less inedible. But I can say one thing on its behalf -- at least it did not rise up from my plate and chase after me with a headhunting sword.

# *An Icelandic Fungal Seasoning*

On a map of Iceland, you can easily locate the Westfjords -- they stick out from the northwestern part of the island like a rooster's frazzled comb. Until the early years of the last century, the Westfjords were virtually cut off from the rest of the island. This remoteness resulted in foods and food preparations that were unknown elsewhere in Iceland. Consider *brudningur*. To make this dish, you throw both fish and animal bones into a barrel of sour whey throughout the winter. By the spring, the bones will have softened considerably, whereupon they're boiled and eaten. Grimace if you like, but a plate of *brudningur* is much better than going hungry.

Even though edible mushrooms such as chanterelles fruit in the Westfjords, locals didn't eat them until recently. But they continue to make a seasoning that features a *sveppur* (fungus), specifically a *mygla* (mold). This seasoning is called *hnoðmör* ("kneaded fat"). Needless to say, you won't find any mention of it in *Larouse gastronomique* or in the food pages of the New York Times.

Here's how you make *hnoðmör*:

From a recently slaughtered sheep, you take the kidney fat as well as the net of fat around the stomach, press them firmly together so there's no empty space in the *mör* (fat), place this pressed fat in a mesh-type cloth, and then hang it in a cool place, usually some sort of shed. After four or five days, a greenish *mygla* will appear on the fat. You allow this *mygla* to continue growing until, as one Westfjords resident told me, "other colors [i.e., other molds] start growing, too." Now you knead together the *mygla* and fat, then cut the combination into 7cm blocks that look not unlike squares of Roquefort cheese, and put these blocks in your fridge or cellar.

As nearly as I can tell, the mold in question is a *Penicillium* species whose greenish color is due to the presence of numerous conidia. During growth, its protein and fat-digestion enzymes are busy altering the flavor of the sheep fat. Whichever *Penicillium* species it is, it's probably closer to *P. roquefortii* than it is to *P. camembertii*, which changes the texture of its substrate, but not the flavor (the *Penicillium* species in *hnoðmör* does the reverse). Not surprisingly, soft cheeses like camembert and brie are ripened by *P. camembertii*.

At my suggestion, my Icelandic friend Lene left out some sheep fat, and soon a mold appeared on it. Might this mold have been the fungal component of *hnoðmör*? Probably not, because it was growing in Eyjafjörður, not the Westfjords, and in the late winter, not the fall or early winter, the period when sheep are usually slaughtered in Iceland. Here I might add that there's never been any mycological work done on *hnoðmör*, and thus its fungal component, whether a *Penicillium* or not, has yet to be identified.

Now for the culinary part of this essay. You get one of the aforementioned 7cm blocks, let it melt, and then put it in a pot and boil it, after which you serve it over salted or half-dried fish and the potatoes that always accompany fish at an Icelandic meal.

It'll also be served over fermented *skata* (skate) on *Þhorlaksmessa*, the day before Christmas Eve. During fermentation, the urea in the skate's blood is broken down into ammonia compounds. To some Icelanders, the result tastes like stale urine, so they moderate this flavor with a seasoning of *hnoðmör*.

Thanks to my Reykjavik friend Halldor, a former resident of the Westfjords, I've had several opportunities to sample *hnoðmör*. Halldor typically serves it over half-dried *þorsk* (cod) and potatoes. The first time we had it, we fell to chatting, and the *hnoðmör* got cold and, as a result, quite viscous, so Halldor had to boil it again. During one of our meals, he told me that an "X" used to be carved on every block of *hnoðmör*, although he didn't know why. One thing he did know: the "X" was not an off-kilter Christian cross designed to ward off culinary demons. If I had to make a guess myself, I would say that the "X" was put there to provide aeration for the fungus.

*Hnoðmör* has a slightly cheesey flavor, but it's very mild by comparison with Stilton, Gorgonzola, or Roquefort cheese, each of which is ripened by *P. roquefortii*. Yet in the absence of thyme, basil, oregano, or other conventional seasonings, that flavor might have seemed extremely tangy to a resident of the Westfjords a hundred or so years ago. Likewise, *hnoðmör* leaves a distinct feeling of heaviness in the stomach. Not so long ago, this might not have been such a bad thing. For in a region like the Westfjords, where there was often not enough to eat, a sense of heaviness in the stomach might have contributed to the illusion of a full meal.

Thanks to Gudridur Gyda Eyjolfsdottir, Lene Zachariassen, Kathie Hodge, and Halldor Hestnes for their contributions to this essay.

# Antarctic Mushrooms

for Bob Blanchette

Should your next mushroom foray take place in Antarctica? Well, soil fungi and yeasts are surprisingly plentiful in certain parts of Antarctica, as are lichenized fungi. Likewise, mycologist Robert Blanchette has found a number of fungi -- including three previously undescribed species -- feasting on the wooden huts built a century ago by explorers Robert Scott and Ernest Shackleton. And I myself recently found a group of unusually large mushrooms fruiting on the Seventh Continent.

My visit did not take place in Antarctica itself, but in the library of The Explorers Club in New York City. There I found a curious tome entitled *Aurora Australis*. Perusing its 200 or so pages, I saw an illustration of a giant puffball surrounded by only slightly less giant agarics, with the caption "Executing Evolutions in Mid-Air." The illustration showed a man exploding like a spore from the puffball.

Several pages later, I came upon another illustration that showed a group of explorers using umbrella-sized mushrooms to protect themselves from an Antarctic blizzard. This illustration bore the caption "Each Sheltered Under His Own Novel Umbrella." It goes without saying that even the most robust mushroom would provide very little defense against an Antarctic blizzard.

*Aurora Australis*, the first book ever published in Antarctica, was published at the winter quarters of Sir Ernest Shackleton's 1908 British Antarctic Expedition, the so-called Nimrod Expedition. Printed in an edition of 300 copies, It consists of scientific writing, drawings, culinary articles, and poetry by various members of the expedition. One article, by explorer Edgewater David, is a surprisingly jaunty account of climbing Mt. Erebus, the continent's highest peak. Another article, "Life Under Difficulties," describes the arduous if not downright heroic existence of Antarctic rotifers.

By far the most unusual piece in the book is a sort of science fiction fantasy by the twenty-five year old Australian explorer Douglas (later Sir Douglas) Mawson. Entitled "Bathybia," it details an imaginary sledge expedition to the South Pole, which, to the astonishment of the sledgers, turns out to be a volcanic crater 20,000 feet deep. Written up like an actual trip, the story describes encounters with (among other things) a six-foot tall emperor penguin dressed in a velveteen coat, giant insects, and giant plants, not to mention the giant puffball and the novel umbrellas.

Mawson, who never journeyed as far as the South Pole, based his fantasy on a dream that he'd had one morning between the first and second call for breakfast. A reader might be forgiven for thinking that he might have had a wee nip before breakfast as well...or perhaps eaten a different sort of mushroom than the ones depicted in the illustrations.

As for the illustrations, they were drawn by the expedition's official artist, an Englishman named George Marston (1882-1940). A large, brawny man with (according to J.P. Priestley) "the frame and face of a prizefighter," he reputedly was fond of practical jokes and dressing up like a woman. He also liked to provide his expedition mates with climatically appropriate insults, such as "Why don't you swallow an icicle so your head won't wobble so much?"

Marston was the perfect illustrator for Mawson's whimsical narrative, and not simply because he was whimsical himself. He had taken a crash course in printing before the expedition, and he was now remarkably good at the job. All of the drawings in *Aurora Australis* are his. He had brought with him an ordinary etching press and reproduced his work by a process in which an aluminum plate is used instead of a lithographic stone.

Marston made another illustration for "Bathybia" (one that wasn't included in the entire printing) captioned "A Giant Tick Was Investigating the Carcase [sic]." Initially, you don't see either the tick -- it looks more like a spider -- or the carcass, because a fruiting of even more giant mushrooms is what captures your attention. In fact, Marston initially had called the illustration "Giant Toadstools."

Neither Marston or Mawson seems to have had any particular knowledge of mushrooms, or even interest in them, but Marston himself was obviously attracted to mushroom-like shapes: he seldom gets credit for it, but his desire to frustrate the Seventh Continent's relentless snow, ice, and winds inspired him, with Shackleton's assistance, to invent the dome tent.

Marston, I might add, made a significant, albeit little-heralded contribution to Shackleton's subsequent *Endurance* expedition -- he gave up his oil paints to help caulk the seams of the *James Caird*, the boat in which Shackleton made his celebrated voyage from Elephant Island to South Georgia. Without this improvised caulking, "The Boss" (as his expedition mates affectionately called Shackleton) might never have been memorialized as a polar hero or, later, an IMAX star.

But I haven't answered my original question: Should you consider Antarctica for your next mushroom foray? Probably not. In fact, Antarctica is one of the best places on the planet to go if you want to escape from mushrooms. And yet, as Marston's illustrations for "Bathybia" show, the farther you get from mushrooms, the bigger they seem to grow.

# Blow, Ye Fungal Winds, O Blow

As autumn progresses, a tree concentrates more and more of its photosynthates in its roots at the expense of its leaves and branches, with the result that when a good wind, not to mention a good hurricane, comes along, those leaves and branches often suffer the consequences. In other words, they might end up broken off and lying on the ground. Thus I found myself following the progress of the recent so-called superstorm Sandy up the eastern sea-board with, I confess, a certain mycological interest.

On October 29, 2012, Sandy whacked the Northeast. The following day, I wandered around the Harvard University campus in search of fungi...specifically, fungi on leaves and branches that had been untimely ripped from the mother tree by Sandy's vehement winds. I found quite a few interesting species. Indeed such was the success of my foray that I phoned my friend and fellow mycophile Susan Goldhor, and she joined me for a fungal prowl of the campus later in the day.

As with a typical foray, I compiled a species list for what I'd like to call the 2012 Sandy-Harvard Foray. I suspect my list would have been quite a bit longer if it weren't for the fact that Harvard's fungally-oblivious clean-up crew removed all errant sticks, branches, and even most of the leaves the day after I engaged in my foray. All those splendid substrates -- gone!! All those fungi -- gone, too!

In any event, here's my species list, with the substrate in parenthesis:

*Amylostereum chailletii* (black? spruce)
*Apiognomia quercina* (oak leaf)
*Botryobasidium sp.* (conifer)
*Botrysphaeria sp.* (oak leaf)
*Diaporthe sp.* (oak)
*Diatrype disciformis* (beech)

*Diatrype stigma* (beech)
*Exidia recisa* (beech)
*Hydnochaete olivacea* (various hardwoods)
*Hyphoderma sp.* (conifer)
*Hypochnicium sp.* (conifer?)
*Irpex lacteus* (various hardwoods)
*Lophodermium pinastri* (white pine needles)
*Phyllosticta sp.* (maple leaf)
*Plasmopara viburni* (viburnum leaf)
*Rhytisma americana* (maple leaf)
*Schizophyllum commune* (various hardwoods)
*Stereum complicatum* (various hardwoods)
*Stereum ochraceo*-flavum (oak?)
*Stereum rugosum* (maple)
*Stereum sp.* (oak?)
*Steccherinum ochraceum* (maple)
*Strumella sp.* (oak)
*Taphrina caerulescens* (oak leaf)
*Trametes conchifer* (beech)
*Trametes versicolor* (maple)
*Verticilium sp.* (maple)

Most of the wood-inhabiting species on this list are unaggressive specialists in branch rot, although a few can specialize in top rot, too. The leaf inhabitors are more or less innocuous except in years when large outbreaks attack most of a tree's foliage, affecting chloroplasts and, in the process, interfering with photosynthesis. Those same large outbreaks can also extend to twigs and branches, sometimes with unpleasant results for the tree. This did not seem like one of those years. Likewise, none of the species in the inventory can be classified as uncommon -- seldom seen, perhaps, but not uncommon.

Of the species I documented, the one that I've encountered least frequently was *Amylostereum chailletii*, a specialist in white rot. Morphologically, *A. chailletii* is a typical *Stereum*-like species, but one of its modes of spore dispersal is anything but typical. Female wood wasps of the *Sirex* genus are equipped with a sporangium for carrying its spores. With their ovipositors, they'll deposit their eggs and a toxic mucus, along with those spores, into the tree of their choice, usually a softwood. A while later, a batch of new wood wasps and their *Amylostereum* symbionts will greet the world.

Since I didn't have the foresight to scrutinize the campus for fungi a day or two before Sandy's arrival, I can't say what percentage of the species might already have been on the ground, but I suspect it would be a relatively small percent -- maybe a few *Rhytismas*, the *Trametes,* the *Hymenochaete olivacea*, and the *Schizophyllum.* A vastly larger number of the species on the list would still be residing in trees were it not for Sandy's powerful winds. Thus only a mycologist trained in tree-climbing or having a binoculars suitable for spying on canopy-dwelling warblers would have found them.

I won't say that the results of the 2012 Sandy-Harvard Foray left me clamoring for another hurricane. After all, hurricanes can have tragic consequences that would offset even a lavish fungal inventory. Sandy herself killed 253 people in seven countries. But I can say this: Sandy's visit reminded me that there are considerably more fungi out there than we tend to observe in our earthbound daily lives.

# Faust:
# A Metaphysical Tale

Rowland J. Faust seemed to have it all: an endowed chair of mycology at an ivy league school, an extremely light teaching load, an enviable publication list, a pair of devoted postdocs, a beautiful cordon bleu chef wife, and so many grants that he couldn't keep track of them.

And yet no matter how much Dr. Faust had, he always wanted more. Here's an example of his seemingly boundless ambition: a while back, he'd written a revision of the genus *Pseudotomentella*. His paper was so well-received that he kept wondering why David Attenborough didn't turn it into a TV special.

One day he was sitting at his desk and finishing a paper about a potentially new Hyphomycete species when he said to himself, Wouldn't it be nice if I discovered a new phylum, not simply a new species? This idea took flight in his mind, until he said it out loud:

"I'd give anything to discover a whole new phylum."

All of a sudden a dissolute-looking man with a sardonic grin appeared in his lab. Dr. Faust noticed that the man had cloven feet and a rank, sulphurous odor.

"The name's Mephistopheles," the visitor said, shaking Dr. Faust's hand.

"Rowland Faust, Ph.D."

"Did I hear you say that you'd give anything to discover a whole new phylum? What about your soul?"

"You want my soul?"

"You don't need it for your work, do you?"

"That's true. I use even a stage micrometer far more than I use my soul."

Mephistopheles produced a written form, which Dr. Faust eagerly signed. All at once everything became a blur. The next thing Dr. Faust knew, he was standing outside the building that housed his lab and looking at a huge purple fungus in a pile of mulch.

"There you are, my friend," Mephistopheles observed, nudging the fungus with one of his cloven feet. "Just remember this: I giveth, but I can also taketh away." And then he disappeared in a cloud of sulphurous smoke.

Dr. Faust kneeled down beside the purple fungus and studied it. It consisted of a large apothecium with a ring of small whitish agarics decorating its margin. Was it his imagination, or did he see a smiley face wink at him inside the apothecium?

The fungus reminded him of, well, it didn't remind him of anything he'd ever encountered before. He collected it and hurried back to his lab, clutching it to his chest. Then he put a slice of its tissue under his microscope.

"Holy shit!" he exclaimed. For he couldn't believe his eyes. On the slide, there seemed to be both asci and basidia. Maybe it's contaminated, he told himself. So he dug out another razor and cut another sample from a different part of the fruiting body, and he got exactly the same result. "Holy shit!" he exclaimed again.

Over the next few weeks, Dr. Faust devoted all of his energy to his discovery. He sent one of his postdocs to the myriad meetings he should have attended himself, and he sent the other to teach his class. He ate fast food rather than his wife's four-star cuisine, and he ignored his daughter's high school graduation, a fact that upset the daughter so much that she spray painted "*mycology sucks!*" on his car. When the family dog needed to be put down, he strangled it. No sense wasting his valuable time with a visit to the vet.

The literature in his school's vast library contained no reference to a species even remotely similar to what he now considered *his* species. Indeed, the sequencing results indicated that it stood totally alone on its evolutionary branch. It was in fact a whole new phylum.

Working day and night, he wrote the paper announcing his discovery. It was all he could do to keep from naming the new phylum after himself. And rather than publish the paper in a two-bit journal like *Mycologia*, he sent it to *USA Today*, which published it the following day.

Soon every publication, mycological and otherwise, wanted to interview him. Shortly after his interview in *The New York Times*, he received a congratulatory phone call from President Obama. "Keep up the good work, Rowland," the President told him.

Obama really has his finger on the pulse of mycology, Dr. Faust thought. Perhaps he'll make me the first Secretary of Mycology. *Secretary of Mycology*. He liked the sound of that title. He saw himself on national television, solemnly addressing the nation about the latest meningitis outbreak.

Before he could call the President back and suggest that he, Rowland J. Faust, was the right man for a cabinet post, a familiar figure appeared in his lab.

"My bad!" Mephistopheles remarked. "I've been looking all over for your soul, but I can't find it. Truth to tell, I don't think you have one. So the deal is off."

"Too late," chortled Dr. Faust. "I've already gotten all sorts of accolades for my discovery. By the way, I think you should take a bath. You really smell bad."

Hardly had he uttered these words when he became dizzy, then fell asleep. When he woke up, his visitor was nowhere to be seen. Nor was his paper in *USA Today* or his *New York Times* interview, both of which he'd framed and put up on the wall of his lab.

Something seemed to be wrong. Very wrong.

Dr. Faust went to his computer and checked *Index Fungorum* for his new phylum. It wasn't listed. He had seen it in *Index Fungorum* earlier in the day, but it didn't seem to be there now. He played around with the spelling, but try as he might, he couldn't find any mention of it.

With a mounting sense of panic, he googled himself. Usually, he got several thousand hits, but now there were surprisingly few, and all of them said the same thing: "Rowland J. Faust -- a fictional mycologist created by Lawrence Millman."

Oh, the shame! The shame! Dr. Faust felt he was a failure, indeed worse than a failure -- he was someone else's invention. And so it was that with the end of this story, he vanished completely off the face of the earth.

# The Noble Polypore

Here's a riddle for you: what's large and furry, more or less hibernates during the winter, and inhabits forested areas in the Pacific Northwest?

I know what you're thinking, and one day in the fall of 1948 Emory Simmons was thinking exactly the same thing. He'd spent that day searching for cup fungi on the wooded slopes of Washington's Mount Rainier, and now the late afternoon light was quickly fading. Suddenly, he spotted something large and furry near the base of a fir tree. His immediate thought was *"Bear!"*

Simmons and fellow mycologist Alexander Smith somehow managed to transport the not inconsiderable object back to their camp; then they placed it on top of the heap of meshed shelves that served as their field dryer. During the night, these shelves collapsed with a resounding crash, and Simmons awoke to find himself staring at what he thought was, again, a bear.

But the robustly strange object was not a bear, although bears were common around Mount Rainier. It was, in fact, an extremely rare polypore whose elongated binomial, *Bridgeoporus nobilissimus*, hints at its incredible bulk. Specimens have been known to tip the scales at 300 pounds and likewise exceed the girth of a sumo wrestler. I might add that *Bridgeoporus*, which was named for William Bridge Cooke, a mycologist and sewage treatment specialist who himself possessed significant girth, is completely inedible. It's also an endangered species, the first fungus ever to be so designated, and thus even if it were edible, you would be subject to a day in court if you decided to take a bite out of one.

Emory Simmons wasn't the first person to stumble on one of these furry giants, but he was almost the first. Just five years earlier two brothers, Frank and Ali Sandoz, found a *Bridgeoporus* in Oregon's Mount Hood National Forest, and that specimen was the first. The brothers brought the polypore to the local office of the U. S. Forest Service, where one employee declared that it was the first fungus he had ever seen that had a "sisal doormat appearance." When mycologists learned about the fungus in question, they began referring to it informally as Fuzzy Sandozi.

At present *Bridgeoporus* has been documented at twelve sites in Washington and Oregon, but it remains more or less an unknown species. For example, it obstinately refuses to be cultured. It may or may not be associated with brown rot. Indeed, it may not be degrading the wood of its host at all, but simply using the wood as a convenient substrate. This suggests that it might be mycorrhizal, with the mycelium living in the soil and invading the wood only to produce its massive fruiting body. On the other hand, it could just be a typical saprobic or even parasitic polypore. But it has cystidia, which makes it atypical for a polypore -- saprobe, parasite or otherwise. And thus far it hasn't been particularly eager to relinquish data about its life history. In fact, *Bridgeoporus* is so reticent about giving up its secrets that it almost seems to be telling us, "I'm smarter than you are."

The idea of fungal intelligence may sound ridiculous (next you'll expect me to say that mushrooms understand string theory), but consider this: according to recent molecular phylogenetic analyses of proteins, animals and fungi are sister groups, with similar motile cells as well as similar mitochondria, whereas vascular plants and animals are only cousins. These analyses also propose that you and the chanterelles you're getting ready to sauté, or you and *Bridgeoporus*, share a common evolutionary ancestor, probably an organism not unlike a present-day marine flagellate. Also, the similarities in ribosomal DNA between fungi and *Homo sapiens* run to 80-85%. This may be one reason why we have such a hard time fighting fungal infections -- fungi are us.

Now back to our giant polypore. To explore its mysteries, study its intelligence, even just to find it, you need a guide. And if you're lucky, that guide's name will be Paul Stamets. If there's ever a Nobel Prize in Mycology, Paul would be the odds-on favorite to get it. He is a mushroom missionary, a man dedicated to the belief that fungi can be instrumental in helping or even saving our beleaguered planet. In the past decade, he has pioneered new technologies that employ fungi ("the world's most efficient molecular disassemblers," he calls them) to decompose toxic waste sites. In one experiment, he cleaned up a site contaminated by a diesel oil spill by inoculating it with mycelia from that supermarket favorite, the oyster mushroom. One of his recent projects focuses on the use of mycelia to filter biological pollutants from surface water. If this latter project turns out to be successful, it could not only be a major environmental coup, but also help cure what Paul calls our "mycological myopia."

As it happens, Paul is fascinated by *Bridgeoporus*, which he calls "the noble polypore." Through tissue clones and spore samples, he's tried repeatedly -- and unsuccessfully -- to culture it. "It's the most mysterious polypore, no, the most mysterious fungal entity I know," he told me when I visited him at his mushroom-cultivating facility near Olympia, Washington. He likened the noble polypore to Raven, the trickster deity of the Northwestern Indians.

Paul wanted to collect more spore samples of *Bridgeoporus*, and so it was that we found ourselves in Mount Rainier National Park, driving through a mist that gave a spectral quality to adjacent stands of Douglas fir, noble fir, and mountain hemlock. Near Nisqually Glacier, he stopped the car and said, "We're in the zone."

Before we got out, Paul made me promise not to reveal our exact location, for it would be difficult to protect such a rare and exotic organism as *Bridgeoporus* if everyone knew its whereabouts. So I should warn you in advance that my description of this site, as well as other *Bridgeoporus* sites in this article, will be somewhat vague.

We began by hiking down a nearly vertical slope. Downed

logs, moss-covered and slippery, gave us almost no purchase, and soon I went flying off one of them, only to find myself draped unceremoniously over another. When not falling off the logs, we circumnavigated their living brethren, some of which were eight feet wide and over 300 feet tall. At one point, we seemed to be lost. I asked Paul if this was a subterfuge to keep me in the dark about where exactly we were. He shook his head and said that Trickster was playing games with us.

At another point, I stopped to readjust my rucksack and, looking around, I noticed that mushrooms were everywhere; coral fungi, delicate *Mycenas*, indelicate *Amanitas*, red-belted polypores, *Russulas*, *Gomphus floccosus*, brightly-colored *Hygrocybes*, Pine Spikes, and boletes—they were by far the most diverse organisms in the forest. They were so diverse and so numerous, in fact, that I felt like revising geneticist J. B. S. Haldane's famous remark: The Creator possesses an inordinate fondness not for beetles but for fungi.

And then we were standing in front of their king.

The world is full of unusual fungi -- fungi that parasitize insects (*Ophiocordyceps*), fungi that can quarry asphalt (*Agaricus bitorquis*), fungi that build geodesic domes (*Clathrus*), fungi that look like squid (*Pseudocolus*), and so on. But I'd never encountered any fungal entity quite like this *Bridgeoporus*. If I were asked to describe it, I would say that it looked less like a bear than an enormous green pizza somehow bred with a wire terrier.

That, at least, was my initial impression. When I looked more closely, I could see that the pizza derived its color from the epimycotic algae growing in the terrier's wires, and that those wires themselves were a dense matting of interwoven hyphae. Also, the pizza came with the works -- i.e., the noble polypore was a veritable micro-habitat on which grew hemlock seedlings, sword ferns, wood sorrel, various epiphytes, and other fungi.

As I was staring at this 36" marvel, I found myself thinking about *Schizopora paradoxa*, a resupinate polypore. Recent phylogenetic analysis has put *Bridgeoporus* in the Hymenochaetoid clade, alongside *Schizopora*. That these two species, the former monumental and the latter quite small in size, could be situated cheek by jowl in the same clade reminded me of one of the reasons why I study fungi: I delight in being astonished.

I also found myself thinking about *Trichophyton rubrum*, otherwise known as athlete's foot fungus, of which I'd been a recent host. Shelf fungus and skin fungus, they're both extremely particular about their respective habitats. Just as you'll never find *T. rubrum* growing on a fir tree, you'll (mercifully) never find a *Bridgeoporus* between your toes. But since there's no immediate danger of a human toe die-off, at least *T. rubrum* -- unlike *Bridgeoporus* -- would seem to be in no danger of losing its host.

The noble polypore is doubly noble, as it grows on noble fir, a mast-straight conifer that smells like Pine Sol. But it grows only on noble fir, only on old-growth trees (a large snag hosted our specimen), only on those trees that have a minimum diameter of three feet, and then only at altitudes of 2,500 to 6,000 feet. What threatens its survival, however, is not so much its exclusivity of habitat as the fact that old-growth noble firs are themselves threatened in the Northwest.

So here's another riddle for you: if evolution rewards success, should an organism be considered a failure when logging practices dedicated mostly to the balance sheet render it homeless?

Paul was running his hand over the polypore's furry surface. "I don't know of any other mushroom that's so sensual, so animalistic," he told me. "When I first discovered *Bridgeoporus*, my wife was a little worried. 'Enough, Stamets,' she said."

So here was a grown man, over 50 years old, petting a mushroom. Or to be more precise, petting the fruiting body of a mushroom. Given Paul's passion for growing fungi, I suspect he would have petted the polypore's mycelium too -- if we had been able to locate it.

"It's difficult to find something that's always running," I observed, referring to the title of Paul's latest book, *Mycelium Running*.

Ignoring my paltry joke, Paul said: "I think the mycelium of *Bridgeoporus* might extend over thousands of acres."

"So we don't actually know when it gets into the host tree?"

"Not yet. But it could exist in that tree -- assuming, of course, that the species is not mycorrhizal -- for centuries before it produces a fruiting body. The mother mycelium itself could be older, much older. After all, there's an *Armillaria* mycelium in eastern Oregon that might be 7,000 years old."

But no *Armillaria* species could ever be mistaken for a bear. Paul told me that he often wondered what sort of potent enzymes the *Bridgeoporus* mycelium might have that would allow it to create a fruiting body even remotely similar to a large mammalian. He also said that there was a chance that this mycelium might be alive and well (assuming, again, that *B. nobilissimus* is not mycorrhizal) in a few young noble firs, although we probably won't know for sure until those trees achieve an advanced age themselves. Unfortunately, the popularity of noble firs as Christmas trees usually keeps them from growing beyond the sapling stage.

Slipping and sliding, we began hiking to Paul's other Mount Rainer site. We soon came to a group of noble firs on whose branches there dangled a wispy green lichen known as old man's beard -- a fitting complement, I thought, to old-growth trees. All at once I heard the cry of *"It's gone!"* Paul was standing next to one of the firs with a glum look on his face. "The last time I visited this site, there were two of them here, and now there's only one," he said, adding, "This is a significant loss to the genome."

Who would want to steal a *Bridgeoporus*? It's not the sort of item that would fit conveniently on a wall or mantelpiece, and its hairy surface would seem to proclaim its utter lack of edibility. Likewise, a rare polypore does not possess the black-market value of, say, a contraband Vermeer.

The remaining *Bridgeoporus* was a relatively young specimen, maybe two or three years old. Not yet having algal symbionts, this one looked like a cinnamon-brown pizza and had a morphology that was distinctly deep dish. Paul set up his spore-collecting kit (sterilized cardboard soaked in malt sugar) and went to work. After a while, he tapped me on the shoulder and pointed to something. There, barely protruding from the base of the tree, was the "stolen" *Bridgeoporus*. Its platter-like shape had made it a convenient receptacle for cone scales, pine duff, and other debris, all of which eventually buried it.

"Maybe there are other camouflaged polypores around here," Paul declared. We looked, but didn't find any.

So here's yet another riddle: had this last specimen gone underground by choice (subterranean insects are excellent vectors of spore dispersal) or by circumstance? Paul took this opportunity to quote University of Washington mycologist Joe Ammirati: "Many a person has stumbled on the grave of *Bridgeoporus*."

In other words, Trickster rules. As I've indicated, even such an apparently simple matter as the relationship between *Bridgeoporus* and its host -- parasitic? saprobic? commensal? -- remains a question mark. Some mycologists think that it metabolizes the fir's cellulose; if so, then it works very slowly, not to mention seasonally (perennial polypores like *Bridgeoporus* usually retreat into a diapause-like state during winter months), and that fir would probably end up dying for some cause other than the noble polypore's desultory devices. By contrast, *Phytophthora ramorum*, the pathogenic fungus responsible for sudden oak death, works with the suddenness of a blitzkrieg.

As we trekked out of the forest, we passed another polypore, *Fomitopsis officinalis*, and it inspired Paul to praise polypores both great and small. Sure, they decay wood, most of them. But that decay gives the soil important nutrients it would not otherwise possess. Their extracellular metabolites inhibit microbes and thus keep them from decaying themselves. These same metabolites inhibit microbes in us too, which is why polypores have long been regarded as medicine on the hoof (many of them are, in fact, hoof-shaped). Consider the Neolithic Ice Man Ötzi. When he was discovered, Ötzi had two polypores in his possession, one of which, *Piptoporus betulinus*, has conspicuous antibacterial properties. His inclusion of it in his kit bag would seem to indicate that he used fungi for therapeutic purposes almost 5,000 years before Dr. Alexander Fleming discovered that the mold *Penicillium chrysogenum* is effective against bacteria.

As for *F. officinalis* itself, the Elizabethan herbalist Gerard described its virtues as follows: "It provoketh urine and bringeth down the menses, purges away cold and phlegmatic humors, removes obstructions of the entrails, and purgeth stools." Likewise, old-time lumberjacks used it as a styptic for dressing axe wounds. More recently, it has been used for bronchial asthma, night sweats from tuberculosis, and as a substitute for quinine in bringing down malarial fever. The Haida Indians of northern British Colombia thought so highly of *F. officinalis* that they personified it as Fungus Man, the supernatural being who paddles Raven to the land where female genitalia grow [sic].

Paul himself markets several polypore-based medicinals through his company, Fungi Perfecti. A friend of mine swears that one of these products, a so-called immune system potentiator, cured his Lyme Disease. I wondered if *Bridgeoporus* might have curative powers, too.

"Probably," Paul said, "but right now I'm just interested in saving it from extinction…"

I wanted to see more noble polypores, for I felt that the more I saw, the less inscrutable the species would seem. So after Paul and I left Mount Rainier, I headed south to Oregon, where *Bridgeoporus* has attained a status not only worthy of its rarity, but also a status rare in a largely zoocentric world: since 1995, it's been listed as an Endangered Species under Oregon's Natural

Heritage Program. Thus each polypore, together with the 600 acres surrounding it, is protected by state law.

In Salem, I met Terry Fennell, a botanist with the Bureau of Land Management, and Tina Dreisbach, a local mycologist. A few hours later, we were driving up a steep mountain road whose multiple switchbacks suggested a giant intestine. Fog and drizzle, the *pas de deux* of Pacific Northwest weather, made it almost impossible for me to see where we were going or even where we had been, although once, when the clouds parted briefly, I noticed Yosemite-like cliffs in the distance.

Higher and higher we climbed, until at last we reached the top of a 5,000 foot mountain that I'll call Polypore Peak. Here the fog had dissipated somewhat, and I looked out on a landscape quite different from the ancient forests of Mount Rainier. There were stumps everywhere, along with cut logs, heaps of skeletal branches, terminally rusted metal, and slopes eroded into facsimiles of elephant hide. According to Terry, the area had been logged until the mid 1960s. Actually, the word he used was "harvested." I would have used a word like "attacked" myself.

"We're going to find a *Bridgeoporus* here?" I asked dubiously.

My companions nodded in unison. "There are more of them at this site than anywhere else I know," Terry said.

Now we began bushwhacking through perhaps the most Amazonian tangle of brush I'd ever encountered this side of the Amazon itself. Vine maples lassoed us, logs tripped us, and rhododendron thickets stopped us dead in our tracks, with the result that nearly every step we made was either backwards or sideways. At one point, I saw a purplish mat of bear scat and felt a sudden rush of sympathy for a creature obliged to find its forage here.

Then, at the base of a stump, we came upon our first *Bridgeoporus*. It seemed to be having a very bad hair day; its fibrous surface was alternately droopy and disheveled, and none of the usual epiphytes seemed to be growing on it. Also, it looked as if it were going to drop off the stump at any moment.

"Once they exhaust all the nutrients from their substrate, they're goners," Tina said.

"What's the life expectancy of a typical *Bridgeoporus*?" I asked

"Twenty-five or thirty years," she said, "although much older, of course, if you count the mycelium."

Studying this less-than-healthy specimen, I couldn't help but anthropomorphize it. For here was an organism that depended on other organisms for its sustenance, like me. Here was an organism whose food-digesting enzymes were similar to mine. And here was an organism that uses glycogen for carbohydrate storage, like me. Now this same organism seemed ready to expire, and I felt like I was losing a friend; a friend who was, if not one of a kind, at least far less than a hundred of a kind.

We now continued our exploration of this not necessarily user-friendly site. Wood sorrel sprinkled the ground like shamrocks, or I should say that it sprinkled what I could discern of the ground when I pushed aside the ubiquitous snarl of brush. Terry, however, was undaunted. He led us through this snarl as if it were his own backyard, which in a way it was -- in order to document Polypore Peak's *Bridgeoporus* specimens for the Bureau of Land Management, he's walked literally hundred of miles here.

"Even though the B.L.M. protects this site, it can't look after each and every *Bridgeoporus*." Terry remarked. "Not long ago, some bear-grass pickers cut up a specimen with a machete."

A few more random acts of violence like this, I thought, and the genome will indeed be a goner But in the next three or four hours we found half a dozen *Bridgeoporus*, all of which seemed to be in reasonably good shape. Each was growing on a stump or snag that was a minimum of five feet in diameter -- mute testimony to the old-growth past.

Gazing at an especially hairy specimen, I asked Tina about the evolutionary logic of hair on a fungus. "It might help with the absorption of moisture," she told me, "or it might serve as a conduit for minerals. The hairs might also produce some sort of exoenzyme. But the truth is, we don't know -- yet."

I've mentioned that *Bridgeoporus* seems intent upon frustrating our efforts to understand it. If we can determine from amplified snippets of DNA that woolly mammoths in Siberia are related with equal affinity to present-day African and Indian elephants, then why should a woolly fungus be such a problem? We don't even need to transport that fungus in a block of ice or protect its meat from the depredations of wolves.

"Well, here's one reason," Tina said. "Until recently, polypores were only considered pathogens, so the point was to get rid of them rather than study them. We're studying them now, but it's like a new science, and the tools are still imperfect."

We trudged on through the choking vegetation. There were no trails, not even game trails, and no other trudgers with whom we could commiserate about the sadistic behavior of secondary growth in a logged area. The skies became leaden, and then delivered a fleece-like substance halfway between rain and mist. I reached into my rucksack for my anorak, only to discover that I'd left it back in Salem. I ended up getting wet -- a not uncommon condition in this part of the world.

All at once Terry announced: "We're getting close to a *Brid-*

*geoporus* that, whenever I'm about to visit it, the clouds always lift and the sun shines down."

And strange to say, that's exactly what happened. Just after he made this remark, the sun suddenly blazed forth from its hideaway in the clouds, and we found ourselves standing beside the noblest polypore of them all. It was fully 56" in diameter and looked more like a bear, although a somewhat compressed bear, than any of the other specimens I'd seen. It also hosted an extraordinary variety of botanical life -- Alaska huckleberry, *Trillium ovatum*, hemlock seedlings, two types of unicellular algae (*Characium* and *Coccomyxa*), several lichen species, and an ericaceous shrub I couldn't identify There were three of four fungal species too, including *Galerina autumnalis*, a mushroom whose diminutive sizes belies its deadly nature.

A blanket of spore dust covered the ground beneath this leviathan. How many individual spores are here? I wondered, and then made a stab at answering the question myself: a number so great that it would make our country's national debt seem microscopic. Yet even that number would be microscopic compared to the trillions of spores one *Bridgeoporus* might produce in its lifetime. Of those trillions, however, it's extremely unlikely that any of them would ever produce a noble polypore in a stump-ridden place like this; a place miles from the nearest living old-growth noble fir.

"*Bridgeoporus* may well be an evolutionary dead end," observed Tina. "It seems to have coevolved with the noble fir, and now that all the ancient firs are disappearing, it has nowhere to go…"

"But ancient firs are disappearing mostly because our species won't allow another species to become ancient," I said.

"It amounts to the same thing, no host..."

But this story doesn't end quite yet. A day or two later, I was back in Washington at a place I'll call Noble Ridge. A parcel of Federal Land within spitting distance of Mount St. Helens, Noble Ridge probably has the oldest noble firs of anywhere in the Northwest. My guide, John Parsons, knew this neck of the woods as intimately as anyone. He was a specialist in fires for the Forest Service, and he also happened to be another person eager to save the noble polypore from extinction.

Less than one tenth of the ancient forests that Lewis and Clark would have seen still exist, but you would never know it in a place like Noble Ridge. The only disturbances were natural -- fires, woodpecker excavations, and volcanic eruptions. In fact, there was still ash on the ground from the 1982 eruption of Mount St. Helens. Walking on this ash, John and I searched high and low for the *Bridgeoporus* specimens he'd found here a few years ago. We didn't have much luck, although we did discover one very dead polypore in a squirrel midden. After several hours of fruitless searching, we decided to call it quits.

The next day I went back to Noble Ridge by myself. I suppose that I just wanted to experience its unusually pristine habitat again. Certainly, I didn't expect to find a *Bridgeoporus*. Walking on more volcanic ash, I noticed something small, russet-colored, and furry clinging to the trunk of a tree. My first thought was -- a bat. Maybe a little brown myotis. But it wasn't a bat. It turned out to be a noble polypore growing on an old noble fir. What's more, its resupinate fruiting habit, lack of algal symbionts, and relatively small size indicated that it was a quite young noble polypore.

I was, in a word, elated...as elated as I might have been if I'd discovered a California condor chick. For here was positive evidence of a new *Bridgeoporus* generation. In a decade or two, perhaps, someone wandering through these woods might see the grown-up polypore and mistake it for a bear. Whereupon this person would know that giants -- or at least one particular giant -- were still abroad in the green earth.

# Chaga's Significant Other

The fruiting body of *Inonotus obliquus* is so rarely encountered that the late Sam Ristich once referred to it as a Holy Grail among polypores. Few mycologists have ever seen it; and if they have seen it, they probably dismissed it as an unidentifiable mass of not necessarily fungal tissue. By comparison, its sterile conk -- the wildly popular fungal medicinal known as chaga -- is quite common. That there's any connection between the two wasn't proposed until relatively recently (Campbell and Davidson, 1938). This is hardly surprising: who would suspect that a cracked black protrusion and a resupinate polypore usually at a distance from each other would belong to the same species?

In North America, the host of *I. obliquus* is typically mature black, paper, or yellow birch -- all long-lived trees. Gray birch, which is relatively short-lived, is almost never a host. Infection of the tree occurs through the trunk, not the roots, and mostly through branch stubs and open cankers caused by *Nectrias*. Like many other primary decayers, *I. obliquus* tends to die shortly after the demise and fall-down of its host tree; once the tree has fallen, its mycelium is usually replaced by secondary saprobes (Niemela et al, 1995). This helps to explain why the fruiting body is found on standing trees, but seldom on birch logs.

The sterile conk usually appears while the tree is still alive, but the fruiting body doesn't appear until after the tree has died... sometimes as long as several years after it has died. So infrequently does the fruiting body grow on a living tree that on one of the few occasions when it did, the incident was documented in a paper (Cha et al, 2011). Fruiting bodies are seldom more than a foot long, so when a twelve foot fruiting body appeared on a yellow birch snag in October Mountain State Forest in Massachusetts, that incident was documented as well (Campbell and Davidson, 1938).

Most resupinate polypores grow in contact with the soil or on the undersides of logs; the fruiting body of *I. obliquus* grows high on its host, sometimes several feet above the sterile conk, and within the decayed wood adjacent to the host's cambium -- i.e., directly under the bark. The only other polypore species that forms a fruiting body under bark on a vertical or sloped substrate is *Inonotus andersonii*, one of the primary causes of mortality among oaks in the Southwest (Gilbertson and Ryvarden, 1986). But you don't need a rope and pitons or a stepladder to locate a specimen of *I. andersonii*, as you might with an *I. obliquus* fruiting body.

Curious as it might already seem, the tale of *I. obliquus* now gets (to quote Alice, of Wonderland fame) curiouser and curiouser: its yellow-brown, reddish-brown, or grayish-brown fruiting body erupts from the dead tree's bark in a manner that recalls the explosion of the miniature alien from the astronaut's belly in the sci-fi film *Alien*. So powerful is the pressure immediately preceding this eruption that the pattern of the inner bark sometimes appears on the visible basidiocarp (Bondartsev, 1971). No matter, because the fertile surface is now exposed.

"Of course," you might say, "a fungus needs exposure to the air in order to disperse its spores." But not so fast. Shortly after the fruiting body has forced open the bark, it no longer looks like a fungus. That's because it's been colonized and then consumed by insects. In Finland, the larvae of the monophagous beetle *Triplex russica* seem to be among the primary consumers (Schigel, 2011), but this species is not known in North America. The North American consumers are doubtless either fungivores or parasitoids of the fungivores -- probably beetles and dipteran or mycodipteran species, along with various larvae.

So while the sterile conk of *I. obliquus* is a perennial, the fruiting body isn't even an annual. Indeed, it usually doesn't last much longer than a few days...a very short time for any fungus other than a thin-fleshed one like a *Conocybe* or a *Psathyrella*. For collection purposes, this is also a short time, since it's difficult to tell that the fruiting body is actually a fruiting body with so little of it left. One of the diagnostic features of that fruiting body is that parts of its hyphae stain dark brown or black in KOH (Boulet, 2003; Gilbertson and Ryvarden, 1986); in an insect-ravaged specimen, those hyphae don't stain because they no longer exist.

Fungal tissue contains choline, B vitamins, lipids, and sterols, all of which are important for the growth and reproduction of insects (Gilbertson, 1984). Yet certain fungi, rather than being passive sources of nutrition, actively seem to solicit insect diners. Think of the Phallales (stinkhorns), for instance. And while many polypores, like other fungi, put up a defense against mycophagous insects, some of them would appear to be extending dinner invitations to them. Several *Gloeophyllum* species possess an odor that makes them a termite attractant (Schigel, pers. com.); *Bjerkandera adusta* is a magnet for thrips; and *Cryptoporus volvatus* eagerly hosts beetles on the inner part of its veil. But with none of these species do insects or their larvae wreak the same sort of havoc that they do on the fruiting body of *I. obliquus.*

"Many polypores are eaten by insects, but in my experience none so quickly as *I. obliquus,*" Leif Ryvarden has observed. Such alacrity suggests a chemical compound that says "eat me" to hungry insects and "be my guest" to egg-laying ones. The insects already dining on the fungus might possess a pheromone that relays a "good eating" message to insects of the same species. In return, all the fruiting body would seem to ask of its diners is that they serve as taxis for its spores.

There are obvious arguments in favor of an anemophilous (wind-spread) rather than an insect vectoring of the spores. A relatively high proportion of fungi that depend on insects for spore dispersal have spores with a sugary slime coating (Ingold, 1953) or ones with spines or knobs, but the spores of *I. obliquus* are neither coated or ornamented. Likewise, the violent manner in which the tissue of the fungus forces open the bark express- es a need for air and thus an anemophilous form of dispersal (Niemela, pers. com). Even so, the unusually quick destruction of the fruiting body would seem to indicate that insects are, if not a primary, at least an auxiliary vector of spore dispersal. For a fungus that disintegrates so quickly might need several strategies of spore dispersal if it wants to avoid extinction.

The rarity of the *I. obliquus* fruiting body has precluded study of its insect populations. Since we don't know exactly which insects they are, we also don't know if those insects might be equipped with any special spore pouches. At the same time, this rarity has hampered study of the fruiting body itself. But rarity is perhaps not the appropriate word to describe a species that typically hides under bark and grows high up on its substrate. A better word might be elusive. And given such elusiveness, this essay must necessarily be elusive itself, a compendium of "probablys," "possiblys," and question marks.

More information about *Inonotus obliquus*, including references, can be found in Appendix II.

# The Cree Upsagan

In my capacity as an ethnographer, I once spent time in the Cree village of Ouje-Bougoumou in northern Quebec. There one of my main informants was Jimmy Mianscum, a large, robust man who was the former chief of the Ouje-Bougoumou Cree. Although he was seventy-five, he did not look much over fifty. A lifetime spent out-of-doors seemed to have preserved him from the worst aspects of time's ravages.

One day Jimmy and I hiked into a mixed grove of birch, poplar, and black spruce a mile or so from his camp. Beneath one of the spruce trees, he placed a bear trap. Then he began smearing a blend of peanut butter and "beaver juice" (the contents of a beaver's musk glands) all over the tree's bark.

Black bears find this blend irresistible, he told me. So irresistible, in fact, that they're completely oblivious to the trap until they happen to step into it. Jimmy will skin the animal, sell the pelt to the Hudson Bay Company, and save the meat for himself. The talons were good luck charms, so he'd kept them until the village minister informed that the use of such charms could land him in Hell.

I was turning over the occasional log to look for fungi. Bears do the same thing, Jimmy told me, although they're looking for ants, not fungi. Sometimes a bear will purposefully set up a log so that it will make an ideal home for ants, he added.

Under one log, I saw some compressed mycelia that looked like cheesecloth. "We used that as a bandage in the old days," Jimmy told me.

And on a nearby birch tree, I noticed several fruiting bodies of *Fomes fomentarius*. When I pointed to them, Jimmy nodded in recognition, calling the polypore by its Cree name, *upsagan*. He told me that *upsagans* were traditionally used by the Cree for the quick starting of fires. At the same time, they provided a convenient receptacle for transporting a fire from one camp to another.

After finding an *upsagan*, he said, he would run a string through it and hang it to dry inside his tent. After a few days, he'd take a piece of quartz (flint was not readily available in his neck of the woods) and strike sparks off it with glancing blows from the back of his knife. As soon as a spark landed on the *upsagan*, he'd blow it into a flame. Whereupon he'd put the burning polypore next to some dry tinder.

What Jimmy described to me was not the only use of *F. fomentarius* among the Ouje-Bougoumou Cree. They also used a smoldering polypore as a mosquito or black fly smudge. Of its efficacy in this regard, I can personally attest. Not only does it work better than DEET, but it's a lot healthier, too. In Labrador, I once walked into a black cloud of mosquitoes with a smoldering *Fomes*...and emerged unbitten.

The Ouje-Bougoumou Cree depended on *upsagans* until the middle years of the 20th century, then matches took over. But matches have their drawbacks, Jimmy told me. You can't use the same match more than once, whereas you can use the same *upsagan* repeatedly. All you need to do is douse it with water and scrape out the charred area.

I asked Jimmy if he still used *upsagans* during his trips into the bush or even at home. "Occasionally," he told me, although I gathered that he used them more for sentimental reasons than for anything else. He smoked cigarettes, and he lit them with a spiffy new Bic lighter.

All of this made me think of Ötzi, the Tyrolean Ice Man. Ötzi was carrying pieces of two polypores, *Piptoporus betulinus* (the birch polypore) and *Fomes fomentarius*. He seems to have used the former to rid himself of intestinal worms. In all probability, he used the latter as a fire-starter, since there were traces of pyrites in the hyphal strands of his specimen.

As we walked back to his camp, I mentioned the Ice Man to

Jimmy. He shook his head. He had never heard of the fellow. Yet the two men, the one a contemporary Cree hunter-trapper, the other a late denizen of the Bronze Age, had at least one thing in common -- they burned polypores.

# The Inuit Pujoaluk

If you mention mushrooms to most Inuit, you'll probably be greeted with expressions of disgust. For they believe mushrooms are the *anaq*, or shit, of shooting stars. This is a not illogical supposition. A shooting star hurtles across the late summer sky with a trail of detritus behind it, as if it was defecating, and there are mushrooms on the tundra the following day. But none of these mushrooms would be considered edible since no one wants to eat the shit of shooting stars.

Yet there's a fungal entity called a *pujoaluk* that the Inuit eagerly collect. Elizabeth Nukarratiq, an elder from Kimmirut on Baffin Island, told me: "In the late summer and fall, we gather all the *pujoaluit* we can find. They have a dry powder in them that stops bleeding and heals a wound. We often use the fluid from a seal's gall bladder to make them stick to a wound...or maybe a spider web. We also use this plant to heal diaper rash."

From a paper bag, Ms. Nukarratiq removed some *pujoaluit*, which turned out to be a variety of puffball species -- *Lycoperdon molle*, *L. gemmatum*, *L. pusillum*, and *Calvatia arctica*. In the past, she told me, her people had special caribou skin pouches into which they'd put their *pujoaluit*.

The Inuit use puffballs both as bandages and as a styptic. If someone jabs his hand with a knife or harpoon, he'll take a *pujoalak* and apply it to the wound. Chitosan, a component of fungal cell walls, will bond with a person's red blood cells, forming a gel-like clot which quickly stops the bleeding. Likewise, the fungus has strong antibiotic properties:[*] think penicillin, which is derived from *Penicillium* species. But the fruiting body in ques-

---

[*] A vastly better word than "antibiotic" is "antibacterial," since it would keep the products in question from being prescribed for viral infections.

tion must be soft, in fact sporulating; if it's firm, it won't have any effect. In other words, an edible puffball is not a medicinal puffball.

I mentioned to Ms. Nukarratiq that *pujualuit* were commonly eaten, but never applied to wounds in the place where I came from. She grinned. Yet another example of the curious habits of White People, this grin seemed to say.

In former times, Native American tribes as diverse as the Kwakiutl, the Cree, the Chippewayan, and Pawnee used puffballs for their medicinal properties. The Blackfoot drank an infusion of *Calvatia* spores to stop internal bleeding. But as nearly as I can tell, the only denizens of the New World -- apart from the Inuit -- who currently use puffballs to heal wounds are the Maya, who collect various earthstar species for that purpose.

Since I didn't suffer any sort of wound during my visit to Baffin Island, I didn't have the opportunity to put the immune-activating properties of *pujoaluit* to the test. Well, I did end up with one wound: I scratched one of my myriad mosquito bites so aggressively that it bled. Not having a *pujoalak* handy, I put a very boring bandaid on the bleeding bite.

# The Case of the Dead Man's Fingers
## A Mycological Mystery Story

Sherlock Holmes was identifying some of the specimens in his friend Dr. Watson's basket. "Ah, here's *Leucogyrophana mollusca*," he said.

"How do you know?" asked Watson. After all, he was little more than weekend pothunter, while Holmes was an accomplished mycologist.

"Elementary, my dear Watson. It has a resupinate, slightly effused, easily separable and merulioid sporocarp. What's more, it's got a whitish margin and...hullo, what's this?"

Holmes removed several blackish elongated entities from Watson's basket.

"Dead Man's Fingers, of course," declared Watson triumphantly. He wanted his friend to know that he wasn't a complete idiot when it came to making mushroom identifications.

"Can you take me to the spot where you collected them?" Holmes said with a certain urgency.

Watson nodded. It was a drizzly October day, with mud-colored clouds in the sky and the maples already a gauche shade of red. They entered the woods, and at last came to a hemlock grove.

Holmes peered down at the dead man, who was missing several of his fingers. "Really, Watson," he said. "Don't you ever consider the substrate when you're collecting fungi? Here you're exhibiting a species of myopia such as I've seldom seen before."

"A species of Myopia? Is it edible?"

Holmes, who was examining the body and the basket next to it, ignored his friend's question. After a while, he declared: "Murder."

"You're sure?" asked Watson. He would have guessed suicide, as there were only *Russulas* in the dead man's basket.

"Smell the basket."

Watson sniffed at the basket. "It smells like old gym socks."

"Exactly... and that smell will lead us to the murderer."

"The murderer is an old gym teacher?" On Watson's face was a look of total bafflement.

Holmes shook his head. "The basket would have been full of matsutakes, the only mushroom with that smell. And unless I'm greatly mistaken, the murderer is my old colleague Dr. Moriarty."

After they left the woods, Holmes got out his cellphone and made a call, then they drove to the local university -- specifically, to the building that housed the Department of Organismic Biology. Down a long hallway they walked, until they were standing in front of Professor Moriarty's office.

"Moriarty has been sequencing *Tricholoma magnivelare,* otherwise known as, matsutake, which he believes is at least forty or fifty different species," stated Holmes. "The problem is, he never can get enough specimens, since there are so many pothunters scouring the woods. So he's now gone to an extreme that I would hardly have expected of him..."

All at once the door opened, and there was Professor Moriarty, his sharp, wizened face peering out from a frame of graying hair. "This is a surprise, Holmes," he said. "I thought your revision of the genus *Fibricium* in the most recent *Mycotaxon* was splendidly done."

"And your paper on endophyte-host associations in Flushing Meadows in *Mycologia* had me on the edge of my seat. But that's not why I'm here. I'm afraid the jig is up, Moriarty."

"What jig...what do you mean?"

"You know very well what I mean. You did away with that poor mushroom hunter so you could steal his specimens and sequence them."

As Moriarty was reaching for his revolver, several policemen appeared and grabbed, then handcuffed him. "Thanks for the tip, Holmes," one of them said. "We can always count on you for help with mycology-related crimes."

Moriarty himself did not seem pleased with the situation. "But my work is being sponsored by the NSF," he protested.

"Tell it to the judge, fella," another policeman remarked.

After Moriarty had been escorted to the waiting van, Holmes turned to Watson. "So let's see what else is in your collection basket, old chap," he said.

# The 2012 Christmas Mushroom Count

Everyone knows about the Christmas Bird Count, an activity where birdwatchers who would rather be somewhere in the tropics brave the cold to inventory the avian species in their part of the country. But I dare say no one knows about the Christmas Mushroom Count. That's because it doesn't exist, or at least it didn't exist until my photographer-arachnologist friend Joe Warfel and I made a late December tally of the fungal species at Wachusett Meadow Wildlife Sanctuary in Princeton, Massachusetts.

I know what you're probably thinking: that all sensible mushrooms have gone south well before Christmas. Not so! All you need to do is lift up a log or two, and you'll usually find a variety of fungi, especially crust fungi. For the underside of that log provides insulation for fruiting bodies in much the same way that a sweater or overcoat offers insulation to a human-type being. Not only that, but the underside of a log is a relatively moist habitat...unless, of course, the log in question happens to be frozen to the ground.

Right away we encountered a *Gloeophyllum protractum* on one of the Sanctuary's wooden fences, *Trichaptums* densely populating a stump, and an *Exidia recisa* even more densely populating a beech branch. All corpses left over from the fall, you might say. Not so again! With moisture or a thaw, most annual polypores will sporulate in the winter (even on Christmas day: fungi do not take time off for holidays), while jelly fungi like *Exidias* can dessicate and revive, dessicate and revive four or five times during a single winter.

The real corpses are fleshy fungi, several of whose blackened remains were in evidence. Someone interested in necromycology might have identified them, perhaps as *Lactarius* or *Russula* species, but I did not include any of these sorry-looking specimens

116

in our mushroom count for the same reason that a birder doesn't include dead birds.

Under one log, we found a fresh *Byssocorticium alkovirens*, a cottony ectomycorrhizal crust fungus. Under another log, we found an equally fresh *Antrodia* species. And on a large maple log, an Asian Beauty (*Radulomyces copelandii*) extended for quite a few decimeters. The common name of this last species refers to the fact that its original homeland is in Asia.

Under yet another log, we noticed a large fruiting of *Polycephalomyces tomentosus* colonizing the sporangia of a slime mold, specifically *Hemitrichia calyculata*. This ascomycete delights in invading the protoplasts of its host's spores, rendering them nonviable. It's one of several ascos known to attack slime molds, and probably the most specific in its choice of host -- only members of the order *Trichiales*. And it seemed perfectly happy despite the fact that temperatures were slightly below freezing.

Both Joe and I were enthralled by this fungus whose caps are seldom as much as a millimeter in diameter. Joe spent the better part of an hour photographing them. Their glistening fruiting bodies gave the lie to the notion that nothing delicate can survive in the winter.

At one point, I noticed a whitish growth on an *Ischnoderma* polypore. My pulse quickened. The growth looked like it might be *Sistotrema autumnale*, a cold tolerant crust fungus species not documented from North America. Upon closer inspection, however, it turned out to be the not uncommon asexual species known as *Oidium*. Goodbye to a first North American record, but hello to another species for our burgeoning 2012 Christmas Mushroom Count.

By 4:30, it was too dark for us to continue our inventory. Later I made the tally: we had found 66 different species of fungi as well as three bird species, two of which were hanging out at the Sanctuary's feeder. And as I write these words, I am eagerly looking forward to next Christmas and its fungal bounty.

See Appendix III for a list of the fungi found in the 2012 Christmas Mushroom Count.

# Foraging in a Volcano

Having investigated fungi in Greenland, I searched for an even more remote mycological destination and hit upon the Azores, a volcanic archipelago owned by Portugal and situated southeast of Iceland on the North Atlantic Ridge.

Let me explain. Greenland, a protectorate of Denmark, has been visited by numerous Danish mycologists, not to mention by such non-Danish worthies as Cathy Cripps, Ron Petersen, and Jim Trappe, but mycological visits to the Azores have been few and far between. Dick Korf and R. W. G. Dennis collected there 40 years ago. More recently, Spanish mycologist Esperanza Beltran and Portuguese mycologist Ireneia Melo made a study of Azorean crust fungi. But that's about it.

The word Azores is derived from the old Portuguese word for goshawk. However hard you might try, you can't fly a goshawk, so I flew a gas hawk (airplane) from Boston to Punto Delgado on the island of Sao Miguel. From Punto Delgado, I drove an hour to the village of Furnas, where I established my base camp at the Terra Nostra Hotel, a facility that suggests an earlier, more elegant era.

"I don't think we've ever hosted a fungus person," Carlos, the hotel's manager told me with what seemed to be a surprised look on his face.

Accompanied by a young woman named Yaiza, the lone mycophile in the Azores, I began my foraging around Furnas's namesake lake. A large, classically-shaped volcanic caldera, the lake has experienced centuries of nitrogen run-off from upland farms, with the result that it's classically eutrophic, although less so now due to the removal of grazing animals in the area, not to mention a recent afforestation project.

Almost immediately we found the largest *Gymnopilus spectabilis* (Big Laughing Gym) I'd ever seen — fully 14" in diameter. When I told Yaiza about the mushroom's effect, she burst into laughter...and she hadn't even ingested any of the mushroom.

There were large fruitings of *G. spectabilis* at the base of quite a few trees around the lake. Also clumps of *Armillaria mellea*, which indicated that the host trees would not be long for this world. Indeed, we found more wood-inhabiting species than mycorrhizal ones, which isn't surprising, given the fact that most of the trees were cryptomerias. Cryptomerias are in the cypress family, and cypresses are notorious in their refusal to take on mycorrhizal partners.

"What's this?" asked Yaiza, pointing to a bluish-green *Pholiota*-like entity. I checked the Bioportal Inventory for the Azores and could find nothing even remotely similar to it. Admittedly, there were very few agarics in the inventory, since no mycologist who specializes in agarics seems to fetched up here. We dried the specimen for the small (35 species) fungarium at the local university.

In the Azores, "where did it come from" is at least as important as "what is it." For the islands are so situated that they're a target for spores from the north, south, east, and west. Likewise, the importation of crops from all over the world has brought mycelia from all over the world. R. W. G. Dennis found *Pleuroflammula hibernica* here, and it has been documented only from the west of Ireland. He also collected *Puccinia pelargonii-zonalis*, a rust known only from South Africa.

Later, in front of the Furnas Research & Monitoring Centre, I found a fruiting of *Diplomitus squalens* on an *Acacia* log. This is a relatively uncommon polypore in virtually any part of the world. Needless to say, it wasn't listed on the Azores Bioportal Inventory.

In a play by Maurice Maeterlinck, a pair of children travel around the world in search of the bluebird of happiness and, upon returning from their trip, find the celebrated avian in their yard. So it was with me: my best foraging occurred on the premises of the hotel. Specifically, it occurred in the legendary Terra Nostra Garden, which hosts (among other plants) 600 *Camillia* species, probably the largest collection of Cyclads in the world, and Norfolk Pines the size of giant Redwoods. What a bounty of mycorrhizal hosts, and what a bounty of logs…

In the garden, I documented the first *Amanita phalloides* as well as the first *Caninus elegans* in the Azores. There was moss everywhere, along with an remarkable abundance of *Laccarias* (Greg Mueller, take note!). Near a trumpeting elephant, or I should say a trumpeting elephant topiary, I found several red-capped *Amanita muscarias*.

As I was photographing an *A. muscaria* button, I heard music. Specifically, Beethoven's 15th Quartet. Was I photographing a variety of *A. muscaria* a whiff of which can bring music to one's ears? Not at all. I soon discovered a local string quartet playing in the endemic plant section of the garden. Apparently, that was the village's concert hall.

Here was an *Amanita pantherina*, here a *Mycena gaulopus*; here was an *Aleurodiscus botryosus*, here a bright yellow *Exidia nucleata;* and here was a typically bewildering variety of *Russulas*. Near a kangaroo topiary was a reddish-orange *Geastrum* species that I couldn't identify. Nor could I measure the spores, since the one oil immersion scope in Furnas lacked a reticle. The dried specimen ended up in the fungarium in case an earthstar specialist ever visited the Azores.

I looked for but did not find either *Coriolopsis azorica* or *Skeletocutis azorica*, two of the islands' endemic species, so I had no choice to come back again and continue my search.

Toward the end of my trip, the gardener's daughter asked me about books on Azorean fungi. There are none, I told her. Any experts at the University? she inquired. I shook my head. How about bringing back Dennis to do more work here? she said. He's long deceased, I told her. Mercifully, she didn't then say, "But how can I learn which species are edible?" Instead, she said, "Maybe you could write something about our fungi?"

And so I have.

# In Darkest Honduras

For much of the 20th century, Honduras was the archetypal Banana Republic, a country more or less owned by the United Fruit Company. From bananas to drugs -- it's now an archetypal Narcotic Republic, with the highest murder rate in the world.

Not surprisingly, mycologists have seldom visited Honduras in recent years. Yet there were very few documented visits even before the country made murder one of its major products. Jack Rogers collected in Honduras in the 1970s, while Greg Mueller and Rolf Singer made a flying visit in the 1980s. More recently, Priscila Chaverri spent several weeks investigating the country's microfungi. And United Fruit periodically brought down U.S. plant pathologists to inspect the local banana crop for fungal pathogens.

I was eager to visit this mycological terra incognita myself, but before doing so, I had to get several permits, including a collection permit and an export permit. Soon I found myself mired in a bureaucracy that was at once inefficient and rapacious. Once

I agreed to pay a certain price, government bureaucrats would raise that price. In Costa Rica and Belize, permits usually cost no more than $50 or $75; in Honduras, I watched my permit fees rise from $150 to $300 to over $600. A government that gets big kickbacks from narcos seemingly expected to get a big kickback from a myco, too.

I cited the so-called Andean Protocol, whereby specimens could be collected, but eventually had to be returned to an herbarium in the country of their origin. As there was no fungal herbarium in Honduras, my citation fell on deaf ears. I offered to do whatever I could to start a fungal herbarium at one of the country's universities. Deaf ears greeted this offer, too. It was all I could do to keep from offering to set up a narcotic herbarium, with dried cannabis leaves, cocaine, etc.

So it was that I wasn't able to bring specimens out of the country, collect in a national park, or collect on public land. Goodbye to growing specimens in a culture upon my return, or doing serious microscopic work with them. Goodbye, too, to my plan to focus primarily on Pico Bonito National Park, a 700 square mile forest that's mostly pristine except for a patchwork of marijuana plantations.

But all was not lost: I decided to stay in a research cabin at Pico Bonito Lodge, a facility adjacent to the Park, and do my collecting on its substantial grounds. Rather than take or send specimens home, I would exhibit them for the Lodge's guides and guests. Maybe I could also provide a few of those guests with a "lifer" that wasn't a bird...

When I arrived in January, 2012, the country was in the midst of a drought. Among locals, almost every other phrase was *muy seco*. I saw only one ectomycorrhizal species -- probably a *Tricholoma*. On the other hand, I wouldn't have seen too many ectomycorrhizal species even if conditions had been more suitable for fungal growth. That's because the dead and decaying biomass in a tropical forests encourages saprobes, not a certain type of symbiont.

Here I should mention that there would have been plenty of vesicular-mycorrhizal species (VAMs, for short), almost none of which ever put in an appearance above the ground. Such species are essential for the well-being of a tropical forest, since they reduce the incidence of soil-borne diseases in plants and trees. Unlike ectomycorrhizal species, VAMers aren't very particular about their partners -- around the world, some 130 VAM taxa are related to roughly 300,000 plant species, according to mycologist Bryce Kendrick.

In spite of the drought, I found a number of wood-inhabiting species, including such common neotropical polypores as *Datronia caperata*, *Coriolopsis rigida*, *Earliella scabrosa*, *Hexagonia tenuis*, and *Trametes lactinea*. The ascomycetes included *Scutellinia* and *Xylaria* species, *Phylacia poculiformis*, and *Cookeina tricholoma*, a beguiling species whose delicately hairy apothecium makes it look like a punk toddler.

Desiccation occurs very quickly in the tropics, which was one reason why I saw such gregarious fruitings of thin-fleshed species like *Marasmius* and *Cotylidia*. Quantity is a hedge against a short life expectancy; with more fruiting bodies, more spores are released into the air before those fruiting bodies dry up, and the greater the opportunity for parenthood. By contrast, a lone thin-fleshed species wouldn't have much luck passing on its genes.

One of my most interesting discoveries was a hypogeous species attached to the roots of a recently toppled *Ficus*. At first I thought it was a false truffle known as *Alpova*, but I later circulated a photograph of it among mycological friends, and it was probably an undescribed species. Alas, I couldn't describe it, because I couldn't collect it. I also found the gray corticioid species *Grammothele fuligo* on the branches of a dead African palm (quote from a local: "African palms will be our new bananas") as well as several *Auricularia* species on the branches of dead or dying coffee trees...a common substrate for *Auricularias* around the world.

Meanwhile, the government bureaucrats were trying to make it hotter for me than the outside temperature. The Lodge kept getting emails and faxes that indicated I was collecting without a permit despite the fact that I was on private property, and thus I didn't need a permit. To the Lodge's credit, they deleted the emails and tore up the faxes, including one that I would have wanted to keep; it referred to me as a criminal. To be labeled a criminal in such a corrupt country -- here was an irony worthy of a Graham Greene novel!

For identification purposes, I used R.G. Dennis's *Fungi of Venezuela*, Leif Ryvarden's exemplary works on neotropical polypores, the two volumes of *Costa Rica Macrofungi* by Milagro Mata et al. and *Common Microfungi of Costa Rica and Other Tropical Regions* by Priscila Chaveri et al. I'd heard that the Lodge had a microscope, so I didn't bring my own. Stupid of me! The item in question turned out to be a 20x dissecting scope. Thus I found myself relying mostly on morphological features in making (or not making) identifications, with the result that the afore-mentioned books were even more useful than I expected them to be.

Toward the end of my visit, I went on an expedition with a guide from the Lodge, a local botanist named Kelvin, and my arachnologist-photographer friend Joe Warfel. We hiked up, up, up behind the Lodge, past overgrown coffee plantations and equally overgrown pineapple plantations, through razor-grass and around liana vines, into primal rainforest. The world became dark not because of clouds or an approaching storm, but because of the thick forest canopy.

Almost as soon as we entered Pico Bonito National Park, the diversity of fungi seemed to multiply. Here was a group of tiny earthstars (*Geastrum schweinitzii?*) on a subiculum; here was a log that a crowd of *Marasmius* had turned white; here was a large orange cup fungus (*Phillipsia?*); and here, stopping me in my tracks, was a trooping of large stipitate polypores. I stared at these polypores and tried to come up with a name for them, but to no avail. The substrate didn't help: in the tropics, most fungi are not specific to specific hosts. So -- God help me! -- I cut off a slice of the polypore and sequestered it in waxed paper on my person. Subsequent microscopic analysis indicated that the polypore was *Amauroderma deviatum*, a species previously known only from a single locality in Ecuador.

At one point, we encountered some stumps -- a sign of illegally harvested timber. This was not unusual in protected areas, Kelvin told me, and distinctly not unusual in unprotected areas. According to him, deforestation was occurring in Honduras at the astonishing rate of 3,000 square kilometers a year. At that rate, he added, all the country's broadleaf trees will be gone in twenty years. Hearing his words, I realized that it's all the more important for mycologists to visit Honduras now, and that they somehow get permission to collect. Otherwise, there will be no documentation of the fungal species that once lived here.

# The Largest Ganoderma in the World

Near Alexander Creek, Alaska, there's a birch tree with a very large *Ganoderma applanatum* (aka, Artist's Conk) growing on it. The size of the fruiting body is not two, three, or even four feet in diameter, but approximately a quarter of a mile in diameter. Or so the Susitna Dena'ina who live in Alexander Creek will tell you.

"A quarter of a mile?" I said to a Native man. "You expect me to believe that?"

"You don't have to believe it, but it's true," he replied.

Reputedly, the large *Ganoderma* in question -- which the Susitna Dena'ina call *k'adatsa* (big birch fungus) -- has powers verging on the magical. If you cut off a piece of it and carry it around with you, no harm will come to you. Or if you ignite a piece of it, the smoke will serve not only as a mosquito smudge, but also as a smudge against anyone to whom you owe money: they won't be able to see you, either.

But you can't simply cut off a piece of the *k'adatsa* and walk away. You have to leave some sort of gift on its cap, maybe some unspent cartridges, maybe a recent copy of *Alaska Sportsman*, or maybe a few coins. If you don't leave anything, you'll spend the rest of your life wandering aimlessly in the bush.

Needless to say, I was very interested in this oversize fungus, so I tried to get someone in the village of Alexander Creek (pop. 40) to take me to see it. Everyone seemed either too busy for such a lengthy expedition, which included a boat trip as well as an arduous hike, or they thought the *k'adatsa* might be invisible to a White Man. One man agreed to be my guide, but only if I paid him $5,000...in advance.

Finally, I had no choice but to play my trump card. *Ganoderma applanatums* are thought to be medicinal, especially in China, where they're used to cure rheumatic tuberculosis and esophageal cancer as well as to inhibit tumors. Indeed, Christopher Hobbs includes a reference to the Alexander Creek *k'adatsa* in his book *Medicinal Mushrooms*.

"I'm suffering from gout, incipient madness, tonsillitis, chronic cynicism, and tick-borne encephalitis," I told a potential guide. "A cup of tea from your *k'adatsa* may be my only hope."

I was directed to the Alaska Native Health Clinic down the street.

In the end, I had to be satisfied with a two foot *Ganoderma* growing on a stump just outside the village. One evening I visited it and, watching a storm of brown spores fall from its underside, I thought to myself: How remarkable!

# Appendix I

## Concerning a Mysterious Asian Beauty

### Materials and Methods

The description is based upon LM's collection on bark on the side and lower surface of an *Acer rubrum* log in Bradley-Palmer State Park, Ipswich, MA, USA on November 13, 2009, determined by J. Ginns (11837, CFMR, FH). Several other collections have been deposited in the Farlow Herbarium (FH). The abbreviation for the herbaria where the specimen is preserved follow Thiers (2010).

The standard mounting media for examination of specimens of the Polyporaceae and allied groups were used, i.e., Melzer's iodine, 2% potassium hydroxide (KOH), and cotton blue in lactic acid. The formulae for these can be found in Kirk et al. (2001).

### Macroscopic features

Fruiting bodies resupinate for up to 30 cm, with spines white to pale luteous, densely crowded, 8 to 12 mm long, odor lacking.

When dry, density of the spines varies from adjacent spines touching to 2 mm between spines. Spines up to 10 mm long, slender, straight, round in cross section, gradually narrowing to a fine, acute tip, i.e., not pilose, penicillate or fimbriate. The space between spines snow white, smooth, glabrous. Small spines extend to within 0.5 mm of the margin. Margin white, appressed, dense, typically 0.5 mm wide but in areas up to 2 mm wide, the extreme edge finely fimbriate. Context white, less than 1 mm thick, dense, fibrous to horny.

## Microscopic Features

Context hyphae 2-4 μm diameter with a large proportion being 4 μm, with a clamp connection at each septum, hyphae where loosely arranged distinct and separate easily, where densely packed they are interwoven, more frequently branched and interlocked. The context surface between spines sterile, composed of a loose palisade of clavate cells up to 8 μm diameter.

Tramal hyphae predominately 2-3 μm diameter, distinct (i.e., not agglutinated), septa infrequent with a clamp con-nection at each septum, typically 45-180 μm between clamp connections. Tramal hyphae in KOH-phloxine reagent remaining hyaline (i.e., lacking cytoplasm), in cotton blue reagent after 24 h pale blue (i.e., weakly cyanophilous). Hyphae at base of spines closely packed and interwoven, walls of some 1 μm thick. Microbinding hyphae lacking.

Subhymenium narrow near the spine tip, thickening to nearly 40 μm near the base of the spines, hyphae densely arranged, interwoven, frequently branched, some segments contorted and resembling jigsaw puzzle pieces. Spine tips acute, sterile, hyphae agglutinated.

Hyphidia scattered in the hymenium, 2-3 μm diameter, some projecting to 10 μm, simple, filiform, obtusely rounded, walls hyaline and thin.

Basidia 29-35 x 6-7 μm, clavate, slenderly clavate or cylindrical with a constricted stem-like base, slender, numerous globose 1-2 μm diameter oil drops, sterigmata four, 4-6 μm long.

Basidiospores 6.4-7.0 x 5.4-6.2 μm, subglobose, adaxial surface slightly flattened, wall smooth, ca. 0.4 μm thick, hyaline, neither amyloid nor dextrinoid in Melzer's reagent, in cotton blue after 24 hours most pale blue (i.e., weakly cyanophilous), whereas collapsed or fractured spores bluing within a few minutes, apiculus distinct, relatively large, broadly acute, contents in KOH slightly refractive due to one large, globose oil drop or numerous droplets.

## Habitat and Distribution

The *R. copelandii* fruiting bodies were growing in the cracks and interstices of the bark of hardwood logs of *Acer, Fagus,* and *Quercus* species. This fungus was previously known from China, Japan, Korea, Philippines, Sri Lanka, Malaysia, and the Russian Far East, where it fruited on logs and decaying branches (presumably on the ground) of *Abies, Betula, Castanea, Castanopsis, Prunus, Quercus,* and unidentified broad-leaved species.

## Literature Cited

Hjortstam, K., B.M. Spooner, and S.G. Oldridge. 1990. Some Aphyllophorales and Heterobasidiomycetes from Sabah, Malaysia. *Kew Bulletin* 45: 303-322.

Kirk, P.M., P.F. Cannon, J.C. David, and J.A. Stalpers. 2001. *Ainsworth & Bisby's Dictionary of the Fungi.* 9th ed. Wallingford: CAB International. 655 pp.

Maekawa, N. 1993. Taxonomic study of Japanese Corticiaceae (Aphyllophorales) I. *Reports of the Tottori Mycological Institute* 31: 1-149.

Nakasone, K.K. 2001. Taxonomy of the genus *Radulodon. Harvard Papers in Botany* 6 (1): 163-177.

Nikolaeva, T.L. 1961. *Ezhovikovye griby. Cryptogamous Plants of the USSR VI. Fungi* 2. Akademiya Nauk SSSR. [1977 English translation titled *Hydnaceae fungi.* 578 pp.]

Stalpers, J. A. 1998. On the genera *Sarcodontia, Radulodon* and *Pseudolagarobasidium. Folia Cryptogamica Estonica* 33: 133-138.

Thiers, B. [continuously updated]. *Index Herbariorum: A global directory of public herbaria and associated staff.* New York Botanical Garden's Virtual Herbarium. http://sweetgum.nybg.org/ih/

## Acknowledgements

Karen Nakasone, Madison, Wisconsin, confirmed our identification of *Radulomyces copelandii*. Ellen Larsson and K-H. Larsson, Goteborg, Sweden, sequenced a specimen and interpreted the results. D. H. Pfister, Cambridge, Massachusetts, discussed the possible explanations for the recent appearance of *R. copelandii* in the Boston area. Kathie Hodge, Ithaca, New York, and Leif Ryvarden, Oslo, Norway contributed insightful comments.

# Appendix II

# Chaga's Significant Other

## Description of *Inonotus obliquus*

### Description

Basidiocarps short-lived, resupinate, widely effused on vertical substrates, with tubes elongated to 2-3 cm; dimensions up to 30 cm x 6 cm, but occasionally much larger; at first yellowish-brown or fuscous, but quickly becoming cracked and dark reddish or blackish-brown; at first somewhat coriaceous-fleshy, then drying brittle; context light yellowish-brown, faintly zonate, continuing without change into the trama; no cystidia; pores round to angular, 6-9 per mm, but sometimes as few as 2-4 per mm; hyphal system monomitic, with parallel, thick-walled brown hyphae 3-5 μm across; generative hyphae with simple septa; contextual hyphae dark brown to black in KOH; basidia clavate, 15-20 x 6-9 μm, with 2 or 4 sterigmata; basidiospores hyaline, later pale yellow to pale yellowish-brown, negative in Melzer's, sometimes 1-guttulate, ellipsoid to subglobose, 6-10 x 5-7.5 μm.

### References

Bondartsev, A.S. 1971. *The Polyporaceae of European USSR and Caucasia.* Program for Scientific Translations: Jerusalem, Israel.

Boulet, B. 2003. *Les champignons des arbres de l'est de l'Amerique du Nord.* Les Publications du Quebec. Sainte-Foy: Quebec.

Campbell, W.A. and Davidson, R.W. 1938. "A *Poria* as the Fruiting Stage of the Fungus Causing the Sterile Conks on Birch," *Mycologia* 30: 553-561.

Cha, J., Lee, S.Y., and Chun, K.W. 2011. "Basidiocarp formation by *Inonotus obliquus* on a living paper birch tree," *For. Path.* 41: 163-164

Gilbertson, R.L. 1984. "Insects and Wood-Rotting Basidiomycetes," in: *Fungus-Insect Relationships*, edited by Blackwell, M. and Wheeler, Q. Columbia University Press: New York

Gilbertson, R.L. and Ryvarden, L. 1986. *North American Polypores*. Fungiflora: Oslo, Norway.

Ingold, C.T. 1953. *Dispersal in Fungi*. Oxford University Press: London, UK

Kaila, L., Martikainen, P., Puntilla, P., and Yakovlev, E. 1994. "Saproxylic beetles on dead birch trunks decayed by different polypore species," *Ann. Zool. Fennici* 31: 97-107

Niemela, T., Renvall, P., and Pentilla, R. 1995. "Interactions of fungi in late stages of wood decomposition," *Ann. Bot. Fennici* 32: 141-152

Schigel, D.S. 2011. "Polypore-beetle associations in Finland," *Ann. Zool. Fennici* 48: 319-348

# *Appendix III*

# *2012 Christmas Mushroom Count Species*

1. *Athelia sp.*
2. *Auricularia auricula (Wood Ear)*
3. *Botryobasidium cf. candicans*
4. *Botryobasidium sp.*
5. *Byssocorticium atrovirens* (Blue-gray Crust)
6. *Chlorociboria aeruginascens* (Blue-green Stain)
7. *Corticium roseum*
8. *Dacrymyces* sp.
9. *Daedaleopsis confragosa* (Thin Maze Polypore)
10. *Diatrype stigma*
11. *Exidia recisa* (Brown Witches' Butter)
12. *Favolus alveolaris* (Hexagonal-pored Polypore)
13. *Fomes fomentarius* (Tinder Polypore)
14. *Ganoderma applanatum* (Artist's Conk)
15. *Ganoderma lucidum* (Ling Chih)
16. *Gloeophyllum protractum*
17. *Gloeoporus dichrous*
18. *Hemitrichia calyculata* (slime mold)
19. *Hydnochaete olivacea* (Olive-toothed Polypore)
20. *Hypocrea* sp.
21. *Hyphoderma* sp.
22. *Hypomyces pallida* (on Tyromyces sp.)
23. *Hypoxylon fragiforme*
24. *Hypoxylon fuscum*
25. *Irpex lacteus* (Milk-white Toothed Polypore)
26. *Ischnoderma resinosum*
27. *Kneiffiella* (=*Grandinia*) *barba-jovis*
28. *Kretshmaria deusta*
29. *Lenzites betulinus* (Gilled Polypore)
30. *Lycogala epidendrum* (Wolf's Milk Slime)

31. *Lycoperdon pyriforme* (Pear-shaped Puffball)
32. *Lophodermium pinastri*
33. *Oidium* sp.
34. *Oxyporus populinus* (Mossy Maple Polypore)
35. *Panellus stipticus* (Night Light)
36. *Peniophora cinerea*
37. *Peniophora* sp.
38. *Phaeocalicium polyporaeum*
39. *Phellinus ferruginosus*
40. *Piptoporus betulinus* (Birch Polypore)
41. *Pleurotus ostreatus* (Oyster Mushroom)
42. *Polycephalomyces tomentosus* (on Hemitrichia slime mold)
43. *Polyporus brumalis* (Winter Polypore)
44. *Polyporus* varius
45. *Radulomyces copelandii* (Asian Beauty)
46. *Schizophyllum commune* (Split Gill)
47. *Schizopora paradoxa*
48. *Scytinostrosa* sp.
49. *Steccherinum ochraceum*
50. *Stereum complicatum* (Crowded Parchment)
51. *Stereum hirsutum*
52. *Stereum ostrea* (False Turkey Tail)
53. *Stereum rugosum*
54. *Stereum striatum*
55. *Taphrina* sp.
57. *Trametes gibbosa*
58. *Trametes hirsutum* (Hairy Turkey Tail)
59. *Trametes versicolor* (Turkey Tail)
60. *Tremella mesenterica* (Yellow Witches' Butter)
61. *Trichaptum abietinum*
62. *Trichaptum biformis* (Purple-toothed Polypore)
63. *Tyromyces chioneus* (Cheese Polypore)
64. *Tyromyces* sp.
65. *Xylaria longipes* (Dead Man's Fingers)
66. *Xylobolus frustulatus* (Ceramic Parchment)

# Glossary

**amyloid** -- turning blue in iodine solutions

**anamorph** -- the asexual reproductive phase of a fungus

**ascomycetes** -- a major group of fungi that produces spores in asci (sacs)

**basidiomycetes** -- a major group of fungi that produces spores in club-shaped cells (basidia); includes all gill fungi and polypores

**conidia** -- asexual spores

**corticioid** -- a group of basidiomycetes that usually have smooth fruiting bodies; often called crust fungi

**cystidia** -- sterile cells on a basidiomycete; often on the spore-bearing surface

**deuteromycetes** -- a group of fungi that reproduces asexually

**dextrinoid** -- turning reddish-brown in iodine solutions such as Melzer's

**echinulate** -- having toothlike projections

**epimycotic** -- referring to the algae, lichens, or other fungi that grow on a fruiting body, particularly on polypores

**fimbriate** -- minutely fringed

**glabrous** -- smooth, lacking hairs

**hyaline** -- colorless; transparent

**hyphae** -- filamentous threads that are part of a mycelium or the fruiting body of a fungus

**hypogeous** -- fruiting underground

**hymenium** -- spore-bearing surface

**KOH** -- a solution of potassium hydroxide commonly used to test color reactions in fungi

**micron** -- one-thousandth of a millimeter

**mycelium** -- the vegetative part of a fungus

**mycorrhizal** -- having a mutually beneficial relationship with a tree or other plant

**resupinate** -- lying flat against a substrate

**saprobe** -- a fungus that lives off dead or decaying matter; the equivalent of saprophyte in plants

**sclerotium** -- a dense mass in certain fungi that contains stored food and can remain dormant for a long time; often underground

**stipitate** -- having a stem

**subiculum** -- the mycelial growth beneath a fruiting body

**substrate** -- organic matter that serves as a food source for a fungus

**symbiont** -- an organism that lives in a mutually beneficial relationship with another organism

**trama** -- sterile tissue in a basidiomycete

**zonate** -- marked with concentric bands on the pileus (cap)

**zygomycete** -- a group of fungi that includes many moldlike plant parasites and insect pathogens

# Biographical Note

Author-mycologist Lawrence Millman has written 16 other books including such titles as *Last Places, Lost in the Arctic, An Evening Among Headhunters, Wolverine the Trickster, A Kayak Full of Ghosts,* and -- most recently -- *At the End of the World.* He has done fungal inventories in places as diverse as Nunavik, Belize, Western Samoa, Nantucket Island, East Greenland, Honduras, a meteorite crater in northern Quebec, and the summit of Mt. Greylock in western Massachusetts. His book *Fascinating Fungi of New England* is the first ever guide to New England mushrooms. He keeps a post office box in Cambridge, Massachusetts.

*Petroglyph at Pegtymel, Siberia*

Lightning Source UK Ltd.
Milton Keynes UK
UKOW06f0216060717

304761UK00007B/469/P